ANNIE'S BOY

ANNIE'S BOY

GARY TODD

NEW
HOLLAND

First published in 2022 by New Holland Publishers
Sydney • Auckland

Level 1, 178 Fox Valley Road, Wahroonga, NSW 2076, Australia
5/39 Woodside Ave, Northcote, Auckland 0627, New Zealand

newhollandpublishers.com

A record of this book is held at the National Library of Australia.

ISBN 9781760794347

Group Managing Director: Fiona Schultz
Project Editor: Liz Hardy
Designer: Andrew Davies
Production Director: Arlene Gippert

Keep up with New Holland Publishers:

 NewHollandPublishers

 @newhollandpublishers

Acknowledgements

Thanks to Mary Anne Radmacher for her poem beginning 'Courage doesn't always roar' and it is used with permission from the author, whose work can be found through appliedinsight.net.

To my friend Gary Stretch who is a born fighter, a champion in life and an inspiration.

To my wife, Jenny who has always been there with me. Love you to my heart.

For our children, John, Erin and Hannah. Always be yourself and be kind in life. Be happy. Go with your gut and never doubt yourself.

This is for the families of the 1970s and '80s who endured and who all have their own stories to tell.

Thanks to New Holland Publishers for believing in our story.

This is for all the children who dream. Never stop believing in yourself.

A special mention for my pal Bobby, who sat with me every night as I locked myself away. As he wagged his tail staring at me, wondering what the hell I was doing.

Alan 'Stoney' Stone. Rest in peace.

CONTENTS

'Courage doesn't always roar. Sometimes courage is the quiet voice at the end of the day saying I will try again tomorrow.'

This book is dedicated to our mum
Annie Murphy
1929–2011

Sydney, 2011

It was an ordinary morning for me, and I was doing what I had always done since I was a young boy, trying my best to punch holes in whatever heavy bag was waiting for me.

My hands weren't what they once were and years and decades of self-inflicted gym punishment, combined with long hours building underground tunnels, had taken their toll.

I hammered the bag as hard as I could, nonetheless. As I moved, the sweat followed me, and the old wooden floorboards looked like someone had taken to them with a watering can.

I knew I had only a few seconds to go for another three minutes to be over and I could see from the corner of my eye that the old guy in the gym was waving at me to get my attention.

As I finished, the old 'pug' stood in the doorway to his office-come-storeroom and he shouted 'Gary, it's for you.'

As I walked towards him, I pulled on the velcro strap and removed my glove. 'Thanks Igor. Who is it?' I took the phone before the old man could answer, and I said, 'Hello.'

I pressed the cold glass to my ear, trying to block out the noise of the gym. 'Hello …' I pressed the phone harder into my ear as I was given the news I never wanted to hear, but always knew I would.

I looked down and a river of sweat flowed down my nose, making a puddle on the floor as I squeezed the life out of the phone. There were no questions, no banter, and no answers to be had. All I could say was, 'Thanks for letting me know,' and I walked away to the corner of the gym.

Leaving the gym, as I walked, the wind and the rain pushed and blasted my face, but I didn't feel It. I reached the edge of the rugged Sydney coastline, and I was numb inside.

It was a grey day as the wind and the swell from the crashing waves battered the ancient rocks. I stood on the edge, looking out to sea and all I could do was throw a small bunch of white roses into the wind, watching them go up and away into the sky and down into the rolling tide of the Pacific Ocean. My mind was a million miles away, but my heart was with my mum in Dundee.

As I looked out into oblivion, the memories came flooding back as powerful as the sea below.

The Roads and the Miles 'Fae' St Mary's to Hell

Dundee 1969

The nursery was busy with children bouncing about as if they were made of rubber, and in between taking turns on the rusty old swing, they were happy kneeling in the mud, making sandcastles and then destroying each other's magic kingdoms with copious amounts of water or one single back hander to end proceedings. Me, I had somehow managed to get my knee caught in the railings of a steel fence. I was four years old, and this was my first memory. It was the first of many tight spots to come. When I couldn't get my knee out, I shouted on the teacher and as it started to swell up, she ran off and called my mum's work. The children stopped running riot and gathered around the fence, and in between sucking their thumbs and asking me if I was going to die or was someone coming to cut my leg off, I stood there like a numpty wishing my mum was there. I remember hearing my mum's voice before I could see her, and as she came bolting through the door, I was relieved she was there.

'Gary, how the hell did you manage that?' I shrugged my shoulders and made a funny face as if to say I didn't know.

At that point, two firemen crossed the worn grass towards me carrying axes. My mum was having none of it and said, 'What the hell is going on here?' and she walked towards the young nursery teacher saying, 'Get me some lard or butter and I'll get my boy's leg out.' The teacher returned with a tub and my mum smeared the butter all over my leg and the black fence posts.

'Right you, wiggle yer knee about and try and pull your leg out.' By this time I was looking at everyone watching me and my knee was like a balloon. I was scared. 'Gary, if you don't pull it out, the firemen will have to cut ...'

As soon as I heard the word cut, I pulled out as hard as I could, and I fell over onto the grass. There was a round of applause from the firemen and the teachers, as Mum rubbed my knee with her hands. The children ran off as I jumped to my feet. 'Are you okay?' When I said I was, she slapped me over the back of my head, saying, 'Wait till I get you home. I've had to get away from work and I won't get paid. Get your coat and bag.'

As we left, I remember waving cheerio to the teachers and as we both pushed on the heavy fire doors of the nursery, the cold air washing the back of my neck as the rain started to fall. My mum took my hand and we walked up the road to catch the bus. 'Mum, can we get a bag of chips before we get on the bus?'

Mum looked at me with a serious face then said, 'You will drive me to drink. C'mon then but I'm getting the crispy one's this time.'

We lived in a small, two-bedroom council tenement in one of Dundee's many housing schemes. There were six families crammed into the block and we lived on the top floor. I shared the bedroom with my mum, and my sister Pat had the other bedroom as she was eleven years older than me. The decor was sparse with basic furniture and no room for any luxuries, but it was as homely as it could be. Mum worked in a factory for years and she would sit at a bench all day using tweezers to put together bits and bobs that would make watches tick. At night she would go and work as a barmaid with my auntie Cath. There were always money worries and whatever Mum did and however hard she worked, it seemed like it was never enough.

I would hear my mum and sister argue as I watched *The Magic Roundabout* on the TV.

'Pat, I have been offered work tonight in the pub and I need you to look after Gary.'

'Ach Mum, I can't do it. I'm going out with my pals, and I've been saving up for it. You can't keep expecting me to look after Gary. It's not fair Mum.'

My mum would reply, 'Life isn't fair Pat. Do you think I want to work all day and go and work at night in that pub? We are struggling and I need to work, and the tenement factor is on me every week for being behind with the rent, and Cath needs me so you're doing it.'

I remember Pat running off crying and staying in her bedroom until Mum was leaving.

My sister looked after me a lot when my mum was working and I have great memories of going into the town with her. She would take my hand and we would walk down to the arcade and she would let me ride on a mechanical rocking horse called Champion, the Wonder Horse.

Mum would cook our dinner in a tiny kitchen that had one small window at the end of the wall, and as she was making our mashed 'tatties', sausages and baked beans, she would take the last draw from her cigarette, stub it out in one of the ashtrays that were strategically planted around the council flat and take a final swig to finish her cup of tea. Before leaving she would always say the same things to Pat. 'Pat, wash the dishes. I have done the pots, and make sure he brushes his teeth and gets to bed at nine. Check the electricity is off and the plugs are cool. I'll be off now, and I'll see yous in the morning.'

And with that, my mum was off down the stairs for another shift in the pub. I would watch the TV or play with my toy soldiers, and I would do anything not to go to bed at nine. Pat would go along with it until I eventually fell asleep or was pretending to be asleep on the carpet. I noticed she always covered me up with a blanket as I listened to the TV in the background. Pat would rub my cheek and say, 'It's time for bed. C'mon. Mum said nine o'clock and it's past that so hurry up.'

I would brush my teeth, splash cold water on my face and run through to my mum's bed to get my 'jamas' on. I would bounce about trying to get warm then jump into a freezing cold bed and wriggle about until the bed's chill was gone. I would shout on Pat, 'When is Mum coming home?'

'Soon, get to sleep.'

'Pat, leave the light on. I need to find my Davy Crockett gun. I can't sleep without it.'

'Gary, it's under Mum's pillow. Get to sleep.'

'Pat, do you think we will ever get a dog?'

'No! Good night.'

Pat would always appear at the bedroom door and say, 'Are you warm enough?' and I would nod even if I wasn't. My sister would turn the ceiling light off and darkness filled the room.

I listened for the key turning in the front door and waited

for a few minutes to hear Mum rustle about in the living room. Each time, I was happy she was home. I crept through one night and as I hid behind the open living room door, I watched Mum sitting down on her chair. As she took off her flat shoes and gently rubbed her feet, I saw that they were badly swollen. She sat on the chair and sighed a big sigh, letting her head fall backwards, falling asleep for a few seconds before jumping up as if she was in a bad dream. She then looked down and began to pray.

'Please God, give me the strength I need to look after us. I'm tired and I want a better life. Look after him. He wasn't meant for this world as he is special so please look after him.'

Mum moved and I turned around and walked quietly along the dark lobby and into our bedroom, crawling across the divan bed and into the warm patch of the sheets I had left a few minutes earlier. I fell asleep wondering who it was that was special.

The next morning I was awakened by the same noise as always. It was Mum coughing up black-coloured phlegm and as her body strained, she clung to the toilet seat, wrenching into the white bowl of filth. Once she got it all up, she would go to the kitchen and have a cup of tea then have a smoke to kickstart a new day. My sister used to tell her off, 'Mum, you need to give them up. It's not good for you to be coughing like that every day, and it's a horrible habit.'

Mum always gave the same answer back, 'Ach, shoosh you, I enjoy it.'

Mum put out breakfast, which was cornflakes and milk, and she would give instructions to Pat. 'Pat, Mabel said she can take Gary to school so you can drop him off at her house. Make sure everything is off, and I'll see you tonight.'

I would follow her to the door, and watch her grip the wooden banister while negotiating the steep concrete stairs. She always stopped halfway down and waved or blew me a kiss then she would be gone. I would go back inside and put my clothes on while eating my cornflakes as fast as I could as we were always in a rush. Pat would drop me off at Mabel Scott's house which was one floor down and she would then run for her bus.

Mabel was a nice lady, and a good, kind-hearted person. I loved going to her house as it was always warm, and she always gave me a biscuit and a drink of milk before we walked to school.

Mabel would have the children huddled together as we made our way through the streets and as we went, more children would tag along until we reached the school gates, then the bell would ring, and we would run as fast as we could to get inside to get our spot on the bench. We ripped our coats and woolly hats off and then sat and waited for the teacher to give us the signal to go and get our free bottle of milk, which was sitting there waiting for us in a blue crate in the corner. I can still remember the excitement of sticking your plastic straw through the bottle top and tasting the milk and the cream that was sitting just under the tin-foil cap.

The classroom was warm as the orange-red colours of the three-bar fire lit up our faces with rosy cheeks as we learned to draw and colour in and the smells of glue, paint and disinfectant bounced off every wall. It was a safe and happy place to be.

We walked home and played in the street until our dinner was ready. Twice a week, our street had a visitor and we always knew well in advance as a bell would ring and we would all stop and shout, 'It's the rag'n'bone man!'

The rag'n'bone man drove from scheme to scheme, collecting anything he could, which was usually old rags, and he handed out balloons to the children with his yellow nicotine fingers. He would then sell the rags to the factories and that would get him enough money for the bookies and the drink.

We would wait at the top of the street and watch for his old van driving slowly towards us and wave and cheer until he jumped out. 'Hello children, what have you got for me today? Remember, the more you have the better the prize.'

Thinking back, no-one ever had much of anything for him, but he still gave us a few balloons and a smile and a wave until next time.

The streets outside the tenements were always alive with the sound of children laughing and shouting. There were children toy fighting, wrestling in the mud and whatever was left of the unkempt grass, small girls were sitting on the steps nursing their dolls and trying to force-feed plastic bottles with imaginary milk into vacant-looking plastic faces, and there were boys pretending to drive a stripped down, skeleton of an old car that had been sitting in the front garden collecting rust and used crisp packets, other boys were bouncing their ball on the side of the kerb, hoping the ball bounced back to them.

I was just about to take my shot at the kerb, when I heard, 'Fight, fight, there's a fight in the 'backies'!' The children all stopped and looked at each other and shouted 'Fight! C'mon!' As we ran, we followed the older boys into the 'closie' of the tenement, and our shouting echoed through the old building until we got down the stairs and into the back garden. As I ran, I had to find my way through the sheets that were hanging and blowing around in the wind and it was then I saw my mum thrashing about with another woman. My mum punched the woman and she fell to the ground, and I watched as they both grabbed each other's hair, wrapping the hair around their fingers, trying to pull out the strands then go for more. They were like two crocodiles in a death roll. I could hear Mum snarl, 'Let go of my fucking hair!'

'Fuck off you cow, I'm not letting go!'

'I can stay here all day so let go of my hair and I'll let you up.'

After a while, the woman untangled Mum's hair from her fingers and Mum jumped to her feet. A man helped the other woman to her feet and I could see that there was blood coming out of her nose and running down her neck and the woman's hair was a mess. Mum had blood seeping through her scalp where her hair had been pulled out in clumps. The woman was shaking, and she was dabbing her nose with her sleeve as she spoke to the man. 'She is fucking mental!'

My mum replied, 'You took my washing line and I have warned you before about using it without asking!'

As the man gently put his hand on the woman's shoulder, the woman said, 'Shut yer puss nobody tells me ...'

Before the woman could say another word, Mum punched her already bloodied nose and the woman staggered backwards, falling to the ground. My mum then turned and walked off towards the steps, pausing and turning around to me, saying, 'Son, dinner will be ready soon. Go and play.'

I looked at my mum, and the children all looked at me as they ran through the closie, and we all went back to being children in the street again.

The grass and the dirt had turned to mud as the rain had been blowing through off and on and there was no escaping it. Bath night was usually on a Sunday, but I was filthy, and the mud was caked in. 'Gary, get those clothes off. Your dinner is ready so hurry up and you will need to get a bath tonight.'

As I sat down at our foldaway table at the kitchen door,

I ate my dinner, and watched my mum cleaning. She was dusting and vacuuming while smoking a cigarette, and every now and then, she would take a swig of Carlsberg special brew. There was Irish fiddle music playing on a tape recorder that was propped up on the windowsill.

'C'mon Gary, let's get you in the bath.'

Mum would boil a pot of water on the stove and carry the scalding hot water through to a big rusty sink until it was at the right level then she would top it up with cold water and test the water with her elbow. I watched TV until Mum shouted on me then I climbed onto a small step ladder to jump in. Mum would bring a smaller pot and she would rub soapy liquid on my head, and with bubbles everywhere we would laugh and giggle as she poured the pot of water over my head and shoulders. 'Hey you, you're soaking the place and me. I think you're getting too big for the sink.'

'Mum, next week, can I go in the bath then?'

'Mibbe, we'll see son. C'mon, let's get you out. Watch you don't slip.'

She wrapped me in a big towel and cuddled me. 'Ohhhh … does that feel good, my boy? Let's get your jamas on and you can watch the TV and I'll make you a bit of toast.'

I can't remember, ever feeling so safe. My mum never said the word love, but I always felt love.

One morning, I woke up with a sore stomach. I couldn't

go to the toilet and it was painful. I sat on that cold toilet seat with legs dangling and nothing was budging. I told my mum, and she gave me two big spoonfuls of warm cod-liver oil for my troubles. I tried to resist, but Mum said if I didn't take the medicine and I couldn't get a number two then we would have to go to the infirmary. I forced the spoons down while gagging on the putrid liquid.

After all that, there was still no movement, so my mum called a doctor out. The doctor arrived and Mum explained my predicament. There was plenty of nodding from the doctor and he then opened his bag of goodies, revealing a multitude of shiny metal instruments, and a bag of boiled sweeties, and as he asked me to undo the buttons of my pyjamas, he listened to my heartbeat and with more nodding of his head and raising his eyebrows, he told my mum he would need to take me into the toilet. We walked into the small toilet and he said, 'Son, take down your pants as I need to have a look at your bottom.' I was nervous but I knew my mum was outside the toilet, so I did what he said. 'Son, I need you to bend over and don't move.'

As I stood there, bent in half, I was nervous at the thought of what was coming next and then I felt this pain in my hole and I screamed. 'Mum! Mum!'

The man grabbed me tight and said, 'It's okay, I'm not going to hurt you.'

At that point, Mum pushed open the door, and as I looked at her, she said, 'What the fuck are you doing to my boy?

Did you stick that pencil up his arse, you fucking bastard? I pushed myself away from the man as my mum jumped on him and she began punching him anywhere she could. 'I'll fucking kill you.'

The doctor staggered out of the toilet and Mum jumped on his back. He stood up straight and put his hands up in defence, saying he was calling the police. 'Get to fuck out my house now. I'm reporting you!'

The man grabbed his bag of tools and left.

'Are you alright son. I'm sorry.'

I told Mum I was okay and as I spoke to her I ate the sweetie I got from the man who stuck the pencil up my arse. After a few hours, the cod-liver oil worked, and we carried on.

It was a Friday night, and my sister was out with her friends. There was no school the next day, so Mum always let me stay up and watch TV. In Scotland, there was a program that used to come on just before the end of the transmission. It was either *Late Call* or *Reflections* and it was always the same. A minister or a priest would sit in a big chair and there would always be a small table and a lamp to give the setting some ambience. The idea was the priest would tell a story about Jesus and his pals and he would somehow relay his story out to whoever was listening, and try and give comfort to the old people, or people living alone. I enjoyed listening to the stories and looking at the funny clothes they wore. 'Look Mum, he's got a funny hat on tonight.'

My mum would say, 'C'mon you, it's time for bed. I'm away to get changed for bed and when I get back, the TV is going off.'

'Okay Mum, he's nearly finished his story.'

As Mum walked into the living room, the priest had finished, and as he crossed his legs, the lights of the studio were dimmed and he would disappear. 'Right you, bed!' I jumped up and helped Mum turn off the wall switches, as she went around checking the plugs weren't hot. Mum was always scared there would be a fire and we would lose whatever it was we had. She stood at the living room door and scanned the room one more time as I jumped across our bed and looked for my Davy Crockett gun. 'Mum, where is my gun? I can't sleep without it.'

Mum checked that the front door had the chain on it, and said, 'Your gun will be there. Try under my pillow.'

It was there, and I gripped it as Mum sat on her side of the bed.

Suddenly there was a loud banging noise and just as Mum jumped up there was a screeching, splintering noise I had never heard before. As I looked at Mum, I saw the door being broken down. Mum leapt forward and I fell backwards out of the bed, jamming myself into the cold, damp wall behind, watching in fear of what was to come. Mum was pushed back onto the bed like a rag doll being tossed out of a pram and it was then I saw him. I was confused, and as he came through the front door into our bedroom confusion turned to absolute terror as he raised a long butcher's knife up while grabbing Mum by her nightgown and holding the knife to her throat. 'I'm gonna fucking kill you!' he said, as he bashed my mum against the wall.

I knew this man. It was my dad. As he held the knife, he moved, and I could see the crazed look in his eyes, his Brylcreemed slap-back hair was falling forward in strands, sweat sticking to his white shirt. I pressed my back into the wall and as I held up my gun, my hand was shaking. I could do nothing but point the plastic gun at him and say, 'Leave us alone. Leave my mum alone.'

My dad looked at me while shaking Mum and, in a flash, he was out through the hole in the door. Mum fell on the floor crying, and then she crawled onto the bed, and I jumped up and cuddled her as she stared at the broken door.

There were splinters of wood on the carpet and a light appeared from the landing, Mabel shouting up, 'Annie, are you okay? Do you want me to call the police?'

Mum pulled the broken frame of the door open and reached for the banister. 'Mabel, we are okay, we'll be fine. Thanks.'

She came inside, and I was shivering on the bed. Mum told me to get dressed. She packed two bags and called a taxi and we turned off the lights and walked hand in hand down the steps. It was dark, as there was only one light working and the others were flickering and buzzing.

Mabel opened her door and said, 'Are you sure you'll be alright now?'

'Mabel, thanks, we'll be fine. We are going to stay with Elen for a while.'

Mabel hugged Mum and smiled at me, and she left her front door open to give us light until we reached the bottom of the closie. The skies opened up as we waited inside the dark, damp space, and as we looked out for the taxi's light, I watched the drips of water from the rain meet and run along the small roof slab making a hundred tiny droplets splashing at our feet. The taxi approached and we made a run for it through the puddles that had collected in the worn-out divots of asphalt on the footpath to the main road.

'C'mon jump in, cold tonight. Where are we off to?' the taxi driver asked and Mum replied, 'Fintry, Findale Street, I'll show you where when we get there.'

As we sat in the taxi, I looked out the window and the streets were empty as the rain hammered down. Mum was speechless, and she had a blank look in her eyes as she stared out the taxi's front window. As I looked at her, I thought about what had happened and wondered, why? I closed my eyes and thought about tomorrow.

The next morning, I woke up in a bed and, as I rubbed my eyes, I saw two feet and a pair of woolly, discoloured socks on the pillow. I couldn't remember going to bed but I knew I was at my cousin's when I saw those feet, and I was happy. It was always a noisy but happy house and there were always children running around. Whenever I visited them, it was like going on holiday without the postcards. We played in the street and there was a big old tree that had a thick rope hanging from the highest branch and children would jump on and hang on for dear life as it took them out and across the flowing burn at the bottom of the hill. When it rained, we got soaked and watched *Laurel and Hardy*, *Flash Gordon*, *The Arabian Knights* and *The Banana Splits* on the TV, and we would have fish fingers, chips and beans every night. I shared the bed and had feet in my face, but I loved it there. I would stay with my cousins and Mum would go back to work and do what she had to do for us. I can remember being told that my mum was coming to get me soon and although I loved being with my cousins, I was also excited and relieved to be with Mum again.

As we left my cousins', Mum told me she had a surprise for me. I pestered her to tell me what it was, but she wouldn't let on. We swung around the corner off the main road and along a short, narrow street. I looked up at the sign saying 'St Fillans Terrace' and as we got out of the taxi, I saw a big van and two men in blue boilersuits carrying furniture through a rusty gate. 'Gary, do you like our new place?'

'Mum, it's great! Is this our own garden?'

'Yes, it's ours. Do you want to see the surprise?'

'Yes, what is it?'

Mum walked in front and as she stepped through the front door, she paused for a second and moved to the side of the wall to let me inside. All I could see were wooden flat boards across the floor and splashes of fresh paint on clear plastic sheets. There was a smell of timber and paint in the air.

'C'mon son, up here.'

Mum took me by the shoulder as she led me up the bare boards of the stair and landing and she said, 'Close your eyes.'

We shuffled forward and then she said, 'Open your eyes.' I stood there, confused, as I didn't know what I was looking at. It was an empty room with four walls and no carpet and no curtains. As my mum walked to the middle of the room, she said, 'It's your bedroom son. We will do it up and I've took on new carpets and you're getting your own bed as well.'

I was six years old, and I had never known anything other than sharing a bed with my mum. 'How can I not stay with you Mum? I don't want my own room or bed. I like sleeping in your bed!'

Mum replied, 'Gary, this is a new start for us. We don't need to share the bed anymore. Just wait until you see your new bed and we get your room all done up, it will be great. C'mon, let's see the garden.'

Mum walked down the stairs and I followed her outside, dodging the two men coming through the front door.

The garden area to the side of the house wasn't grassed, nor did it have any flowers bursting with colour. It was a patch of council land that was a jungle of grey and brown bushes with spiky nettles. I loved it and my imagination took over and ran as wild as the weeds in the ground. As the men finished and laid down the last box, Mum handed them a can of lager each and the corned beef sandwiches she had made them. I watched them scoff them down as they gathered their hessian cloth sheets before leaving.

Mum had two pies in the oven and as we waited on them heating up, we unpacked some boxes of ornaments and ashtrays. There were small toby jugs that had faces of old pirates from through the years that my mum had collected and meticulously arranged around our new living room. There was an armchair and a matching settee that sat alongside the big window that looked out to the street and a full view of the washing lines of the run-down tenements across the 'backies'. Mum had 'taken on' a new wooden mantelpiece that sat against the wall next to the TV, and a two-bar fire that lit up with an orange glow giving the illusion that there were burning hot coals smouldering within the metal frame.

I remember Mum telling my sister that she took on a lot of 'tick' buying new carpets and furniture as this was going to be new stuff for a new start for us and she would pay it off in a few years' time.

We sat at the front door, ate our pies and threw flaky

crumbs to the birds as they pecked, hopped, and swallowed, then flew off.

That night, it was the strangest feeling. As I lay in my own bed, in my own room, a feeling of panic started to overwhelm me. I knew my mum was right next door and as I looked around, it was like I was lying in this huge box. Then, just when I needed her, she appeared. 'C'mon you, get to sleep. Move over and let me in and no farting.'

As she tickled me, we both laughed, and I can't remember falling asleep.

The next day we went for a walk to find the shops and Mum stopped to talk to the women in the street. Each time we stopped I would listen to the conversations. Some of the women had children hanging off them and there were girls and boys standing staring at me, saying nothing. As I stood there wishing Mum would stop talking, I was fixated on a small boy who had his arm wrapped around his mum's leg, clinging to her. He looked bald but wasn't and he had a big, egg-shaped bump on his head and a crusty, runny nose that was dribbling into his mouth. As he stared at me, he screwed up his old-man face and lapped up the 'snotters' with the tip of his tongue.

Although I had already heard the story, my mum said, 'That woman's other wee boy cannie get the toilet. Two weeks now. I told his mum she should get up to the doctors. That's no good. See Gary, cod-liver oil and prunes keep you regular son.'

I looked up at Mum and said 'Yeah Mum. If there is a chipper, can we get a bag o' chips?'

'Let's see what's there and we'll see when we get there.'

As we walked along the streets, I noticed there were houses with wooden boards covering the windows, and there were old, rusted cars sitting in front gardens, with missing wheels and axles, propped up on bricks, and windows smashed in and black plastic taped around the doors. There was the noise of dogs barking, and they had been and gone and had left shite everywhere along the footpaths, and rubbish and sweetie papers were swirling and blowing in the wind as we reached the shops.

There was a chipper, and we did share a bag of chips. As we walked up the hill, we counted the number of boards on the windows and, miraculously, we avoided stepping in dog shit.

When we got home, Mum vacuumed the newly laid carpet and I played in the garden with my toy soldiers. I was busy digging out a trench for my soldiers, which was going to be a river that separated the cowboys from the US marines in an epic battle later that day.

I looked along the street and saw a car coming towards the garden. I recognised the driver and dropped my digging stick and ran inside. 'Mum, we need to hide. It's him! Hurry, he'll be here in a minute.'

Mum turned off the vacuum cleaner and said, 'Gary, it's

okay. I know. I know. I was going to tell you. Me and your dad are getting back together. I spoke to your dad. It's okay.'

I heard the rusty gate squeaking and then footsteps on the gravel path which led to our front door. Mum walked out of the living room and I was right behind her as she opened the door.

'Hi Bert. C'mon in … do you want a cup o' tea?'

As he walked in, I thought back to the last time I saw him. He looked very different. He was dressed in a pair of grey pants and a black dress jacket with a white shirt. His hair was swooshed back and wet looking and he was quiet and smiling. I could see part of a white string vest poking out the top of his shirt and he smelt of Old Spice.

I remembered him thrashing my mum around and I remembered Mum's motionless body, lying on the bed as I cradled her while I held my gun, and I remembered the rage and anger in his face. It was hard not to remember and impossible to forget.

'No, not for me Annie. I thought I would drop in to see how you and Gary were doing.'

And Mum said, 'We have been fine. We're okay … eh Gary?'

I didn't say anything. My dad looked at me and Mum and said, 'You've got the place looking fine. Is this a new carpet?'

'Yes, we've settled in, and the neighbours are great.'

As Dad sat down, he looked over at me and he looked

around the living room and said, 'So how are you getting on at school?'

'It's okay. When I went back, they didn't like my hair and they said I had to get it cut.'

'Ach, don't worry about them son … Annie, I need to get going as I have a few things to do.'

Mum looked at me as my dad stood up. He then rubbed the top of my head, and I can remember jumping and pulling back my head. 'See you son. Be good for your mum and I'll see you soon.'

I didn't answer him, and I turned around and watched the TV. My silence was my defence, and I was glad he was leaving but at the same time I wondered where he was going.

The front door closed, and Mum walked into the kitchen and turned on the tap. I stopped watching the TV and asked, 'Is he going to hit you again?'

Mum turned the tap off and said, 'No … No he won't. He loves you and me, and everything will be fine. We will stay here, and we will go down to your dad's house on the weekends and he will pick you up if I have to work in your Auntie Cath's pub. This will be a new start for us.' Mum went back to washing the dishes and I returned to my jungle.

The rest of the afternoon, there were battles going on in my head and I decided to let the cowboys and Indians beat the marines, and the river I made eventually caved in and there were casualties and lost soldiers in the mud, and trails of shit everywhere. As the darkness closed in outside, I looked at our front door and I thought about the battles to come.

The house was eerily quiet that night and as I lay in my bed, I heard Mum praying and I listened as always.

'Please God. Keep us safe. We need a break. A new start. Life has been shite for him. Sorry for swearing. Can you look after my boy? I know I ask the same thing all the time. While I'm here God, I met a woman today and she told me her wee boy Patsy cannie get the toilet so I was wondering if you could help him go. She was really worried about him. That would be great if you could help him. Thanks, Amen.'

I drifted off thinking about my dad, and the boy that couldn't get the toilet, and his brother with the old man's face, licking his snot.

ANIMALS

My mum continued working in the factory and the pub, and I went to school and played war games in the bushes. At weekends, we would pack a small bag and I would take my school bag filled with crayons, my toy gun and soldiers and we would catch the bus down to my dad's house. I would play in his 'backies', climbing the trees trying to find bird nests, and we would watch the boxing on the black-and-white TV.

I have memories of sitting on my dad's knee eating sweeties, and watching Ken Buchanan beat Jim Watt and Ken Norton breaking Muhammad Ali's jaw, as my dad lifted his arm up, squeezing his fist and tensing up his left bicep, saying, 'Look Gary, feel how strong they are.'

Even now, all these years later, I can still smell the stale beer that wafted through his house when he would make homemade bread and I remember him leaving the house and not coming back until it was time for us to go home again. It seemed he always had somewhere to be other than with us and when he did come back, he would always be bringing home stuff in big cardboard boxes, and old furniture, and even animals.

One Saturday morning, Mum was making me a sandwich in the kitchen and suddenly there was a knock at the door, and I could hear my dad coming down the stairs. 'Alright, okay, hold on, I'm coming.'

Through the leafy, frosted glass door I could see two black figures. I watched as Dad swung open the front door. There were two policemen standing, stone faced, with their legs apart and their arms behind their backs. 'Are you Bert?'

'You know who I am, what do you want?'

The policeman said, 'Where did you get the horse?'

I looked through the living room door and out the big windows and, to my surprise, there was a horse standing in the front garden.

Dad answered, 'What horse? That's not a horse, Sherlock, it's a pony.'

The two policemen looked at each other and the other policeman said, 'Don't get fucking smart with us. We'll ask you again, where did you get the pony?'

'I don't know how it got there. There's a pony shop down the road that sells ponies so maybe it came from there? It's not mine.'

The policeman stepped forward a bit and said, 'It's in your garden and you are saying you didn't see it?'

Dad stepped back a bit and said, 'The only thing I see is one pony and two horses' arses and none of you should be here, now fuck off!'

The two policemen made a move and said, 'Right you, you're coming with us.'

The policemen tried to grab his arms, but they missed, and Dad clocked the policeman with a left right cross that sent his jaw twisting around and he collapsed to the concrete slab. The other policeman tackled Dad around the waist and they both fell to the floor, wrestling between the door and a pile of boxes that had arrived the night before. Mum pulled me in close to her but there was nowhere to go. Just as Dad rolled on top of the policeman, the other one got to his feet and kicked him in the face, and once he got his attention, he stomped on the side of his head. They pulled him outside and they both took turns kicking what fight he had left in him, and they dragged him out through the steel gate and into the back doors of their van. I looked at Mum and she didn't say anything. We sat down and ate our sandwich, and as we looked out the open front door, and into the garden, we watched the cars zoom past on the main road and we could see the pony eating the neighbours' flowers as the sun burst through the clouds.

Another time, I was drawing at the small coffee table in the living room, and Mum was sitting in the armchair sewing, and Dad walked in the door after being out all day. He was wearing a pair of chocolate-brown pants and he had on a white string vest that was covered with red dribbles and spots across his chest. Mum jumped up and she ushered him out to the kitchen. When she returned, I asked her what the red stains were and if they were blood. Mum replied, 'No son, it's not blood. It's tomato sauce.' From there on in, or at least for a while, I thought my dad was a messy eater.

The winter that year was freezing and, to make things worse, there was a shortage of coal as the miners had gone on strike and the pits of Scotland and the north of England had closed. The streets were dark, and each school handed out high-vis elastic armbands that fitted over your duffel coat. The idea was to make children walking to and from school more visible and reflective to the traffic trying to navigate through the darkness and the blizzards. We had boxes of white candles and there was a candle melted onto a small plate burning in every room in every house. When you were out in the street playing, all you saw were rooms in darkness, and a flickering light and shadows jumping in peoples' windows.

It was cold inside so the streets were filled with children running about, playing hide and seek, and there were small bonfires blazing in the backies. The older kids would scare the shite out of the 'bairns', telling them ghost stories as they sat huddled together, burning wood inside forty-four gallon drums, as they rubbed their palms together with the flames licking the tips of their tingling hands.

Each child was wide-eyed and caught in the moment as the older boy started to tell the tale. Children were fixated on the boy as he stood there with the orange flames surrounding his black figure, making his face glow and look menacing as he spoke. 'Here is the tale of "The Severed Hand" that would lie dormant, rotting away, year after year. Every winter in Dundee, it would come back to life hoping to find a home and a wee boy or girl, and it would crawl along the streets searching for children. It would follow them home and the hand would then climb up their bed and under their covers …'

As the boy was telling the story, none of us noticed another boy who had slipped out into the darkness and, unbeknown to us, was getting ready to pounce as his pal came to his climactic finish.

'… and as the withered hand scratched and clung to the wooden bed as it moved its pointed fingers towards the child's …'

At that point, the older boy shouted 'throat' and the other boy jumped out of the darkness and grabbed one of the street children's necks and there was panic and screaming. There were children running down the road, running in panic, running anywhere, and then stopping dead in their tracks once they heard the two boys laughing.

The boy that was grabbed said, 'Bastard … you fucking

bastards. You could have gave me a heart attack. That's no funny. I'm telling my mum on you.'

He then ran off and everyone laughed and the older boy laughed and said, 'Ach, it was only a joke. Stop being a fanny you.'

It was funny. I was just glad he didn't grab me.

The worst thing, other than being cold in the house, was the silence. There was nothing to do and I would draw and colour in using the candlelight. I wondered when our telly and the fire would be coming back on. I complained to Mum that I was cold and asked when I'd be able to watch *Scooby-Doo* again and she smiled and said, 'Gary, I'm cold. Everybody is. We will be okay. It's hard to tell but I'll try to explain what's going on. We need coal to give us electricity, which we need to get the fire and the TV working. The coal miners are not getting coal for us because they have been treated badly at work and they decided to stop work until they get treated better. Hopefully they do, and we will get warm again and you can watch *Scooby-Doo*.'

The same day, I was going to the shops with Mum and, as usual, she stopped to speak with the other women in the street. 'Hi Annie, fucking cold, eh? Wait till you hear this one. This is a topper. You know blonde Jeanie, three doors down? Well Peggy saw the coal man turning up in his truck and you know how short on coal we are? Jeanie waved at him from her doorstep, and he carried in a big bag of coal and put it in her bin at the back. He went into that 'hoose'

and was in there for two hours. Two fucking hours Annie!
Peggy heard noises and the curtains were closed. Jeanie is
shagging the coal man to keep her bairns warm. What about
that then?'

Mum shook her head and said, 'What a bastard, taking
advantage of that poor woman. Hopefully they boys down
the pits get back to work soon eh. I need to get going. See
you later on. C'mon Gary.'

As we walked down the road, I waited for Mum to say
something about the conversation she just had, but this time
she didn't say anything. As usual, I had heard it anyway.
We walked through the wet slush, and the icy puddles were
cracking and trapped water was overflowing and running
down the drains. It was around four o'clock and it was
starting to get dark and the temperature was dropping as
we turned the corner; and then something happened. After
a month of darkness, lights appeared in windows, and we
could hear people cheering in unison for miles around.

The snow was gone, piles of ice were scattered along the
fences and the rain was blowing as we stepped off the bus.
We walked to Dad's house and as soon as we arrived, he
was out the door saying, 'I'll be home soon. I have a few
things to do.'

The fire was on, and we watched the TV, then Mum
took me upstairs where I would sleep in a room that had a

double bed with big nobs on its four corner posts. There was a smell of dampness, and it was always cold. I positioned my toy soldiers on imaginary hills that were on the bed, and I would listen for Dad coming home and hope there was no shouting.

I always snuck through in the middle of the night as I got scared in that room. I jumped in my mum's side of the bed but would usually end up in the middle, between the two of them. It was uncomfortable as Dad slept on a door, saying it was good for his back, and I was sleeping on the edge of his door. Although it wasn't comfy, it was better than being in that damp room with all the shadows.

The next morning, Mum made breakfast, which was black pudding, eggs and toast. That's what he liked. We were going on a drive in a car Dad had bought, and he wanted to try it out on the motorway. I was watching *Quatermass and the Pit* on the TV and we had our breakfast while the film was on.

It was still cold but the sun was shining, and I stuck my head out the back window and my long hair was blasted back as we raced down the motorway. On the way back, we stopped off at a farm and Dad introduced Mum and me to a big man called Andy who said he was going to buy a bear called Hercules, and he said I could come back and visit him one day. I remember being so excited at the thought of meeting a real bear. Dad shook the man's hand then we left.

Dad asked me if I wanted an ice cream and we drove into

a motorway cafe. I remember there being a line and there were too many choices for an eight-year-old, and every photo on the board looked great. There was a knickerbocker glory, banana boat, chocolate sundaes and regular ice creams. I couldn't choose. Dad said, 'What do you want Annie?'

'I'll have the vanilla cone, Bert. What are you wanting Gary?'

'Can I get the knickerbocker glory?'

Dad looked at the board and said, 'Are you sure you don't want the same as your mum?'

'No, can I have that? I've never had one before.'

Dad looked at the board again then ordered. We sat at one of the booths and our ice creams arrived. I sat there looking at the big glass with strawberry sauce running down the outside and as I pulled out the long spoon, I tasted the cream and it tasted horrible. I dug down into the ice cream and I had another go and panic set in as I knew that I couldn't swallow any of it. Mum was looking at her cone as she licked it and Dad had finished his and was looking out the cafe's window. 'Mum, I don't like it. I can't eat it.'

Mum looked at me and Dad said, 'That cost me a fortune and you've not even tried it. Try it!'

I was nervous and the thought of taking a spoonful was making me feel sick. 'I have tried it Mum. I tried it when you weren't looking. I can't eat it.'

Mum was looking at me and motioning to me to have a

try. 'Gary, have one spoonful. It's okay if you don't like it son.'

Dad said, 'Like fuck it's okay. He asked for that so he's eating it.'

I felt sick, and I was nervous, and I wondered what was going to happen next. 'Bert, he's a wee boy. C'mon, let's go.'

As Mum stood up, he grabbed her coat sleeve and said, 'Sit down and shut yer puss. He is eating this.' I started to cry, and Dad grabbed the spoon and rammed the ice cream into my mouth, saying, 'Fucking eat it.' His eyes were staring at me as he forced another spoon into my mouth and there was ice cream going everywhere. Mum tried to grab Dad's arms and the people in the cafe were all looking over at us. I was crying and looking at my mum grabbing my dad around his neck as he force fed me. I ended up being sick all over the table and the linoleum floor. Mum was shouting at him, and the manager woman came over and told us to leave.

When we got outside, Mum took hold of me and called my dad for everything under the sun. We got washed at the motorway cafe's toilet and as we drove back up the road, the car was quiet, and I looked out the window and thought about meeting the bear. When we arrived at Dad's house, we got out the car, and Mum grabbed our bags and we walked up the road to get the bus home.

Other than the usual early morning wake up coughing

routine, I noticed Mum had been spending more time in the toilet.

It sounded as if she was being sick or trying to be sick and I would stand outside the locked door and ask her if she was okay. 'I'm okay son. I must have eaten something that doesn't agree with me. Go and play. I'm okay.' When she would appear, I would ask her again and she always blamed it on the mince or the stew she had made for the previous night's dinner. I would leave the living room and go to the toilet to see if there was anything, and I saw a kind of yellow oil floating and sticking to the edge of the pan, and I would flush the bile away.

I had to go down to the Timex factory to meet Mum at work, as she had to go to the doctor's. There was a big window in the foyer of the building and whenever I was waiting for her, I would look through at the women sitting at the benches working.

As I watched, I saw two women arguing and shouting and they were pointing their fingers at each other. 'It's my turn tonight. I need the overtime more than you, as you have a man.'

The woman was chewing gum and she replied, 'It's not your night, it's mine, and we all need the money.'

The other woman said, 'Fuck off Eileen, your man earns good money.'

The woman stopped chewing and said, 'Listen here you cow, I can't help if you can't keep a man,' and as I sat there watching, the woman went mental and tried to grab anything she could. She wrapped her fist around the other woman's hair and a vicious fight broke out, and I had a ringside seat, looking through the glass. The gaffer got involved and as he tried to step in to break them up, the girl chewing the gum grabbed his wig and it ripped off in her hand. I was laughing and then the woman's bra came off and I was amazed as her breast popped out of her buttoned-up overalls.

As I stood there, staring at her plump breast, Mum grabbed my arm and said, 'Right you, enough of that. Let's go.'

'Mum, I saw that woman naked.'

'No you never. C'mon, let's get some chips before we get the bus.'

We walked to the chipper, and we shared our chips. As we sat on the wall outside the shops, I was trying to fish the crispy chips from the soggy, vinegar-covered newspaper, and Mum said, 'I need to find somewhere for you to go after school. You can't keep coming down here and you can't go home on your own so me and your dad were thinking you could go to his auntie's for a while.'

I stopped eating and said, 'Why can't I go home or go down to Dad's house?'

'Gary, your dad won't be in, and I don't want you putting on electricity and being there on your own. I need to work, and I need your help with this. We have no choice just now, and anyway, I think they have a dog.'

I grabbed the last crispy chip and said, 'Okay, I'll go.'

Mum took the wet newspaper wrapping and said, 'It will be fine. It's only for a wee while. C'mon, let's get the bus.'

The school bell rang and we all ran out the school gates. I watched the other boys and girls walking up the road to get home as I stood waiting for the bus, and I wished I could just keep walking. The wind was freezing as I stepped off the bus and I could feel it pushing me back as I rounded the corner to find my dad's auntie's house. I followed the numbers on the gates and front doors, and I saw the number ten and walked up the path and stood on the top step, but I couldn't reach the knocker, so I knocked on the door. Immediately, the door opened. There was a tall old man with a long white moustache, and he was wearing a grandad-type striped shirt and he was holding his braces in his hands. 'You must be Gary. I'm Jim. Come in.'

I stepped inside the house and said, 'Yes, I'm Gary. Bert's son.'

I walked into the living room and the room was dark. All the windows were blacked out by black curtains and there was the combined smell of dampness, wet dog hair, and pipe tobacco. A fire was blazing behind a steel cage under the mantelpiece. I sat down on the edge of an old settee, and Jim sat down on his chair and gazed into the fire, saying nothing, as he stroked his facial hair like it was his favourite animal, and sucked in on his pipe. His eyes lowered as he puffed and packed the tobacco in, and every now and then, he would spit into the fire wall, and it would sizzle and bubble before it fell into the coals below.

Fifteen minutes went by, and a thin woman appeared from the kitchen. She looked as if she was out of breath and had the look on her face as if she was late for something. 'You must be Gary. I'm your Auntie Helen. I'm ...'

Jim butted in and shouted, 'He knows who you are you stupid woman!'

Helen smiled then said, 'Would you like a biscuit? I have a lot of old comics for you. Do you want to see the dog?'

Jim coughed a big cough as he was trying to say something, then said, 'Woman, leave him be. He's just here and you're pestering him.'

Helen motioned for me to follow her to the kitchen, and she reached up for the tin of biscuits. She prised and popped the lid and the biscuits looked older than Jim's moustache, but I took one anyway. Auntie Helen opened the back door and a cold breeze blew through the kitchen. 'Get that door closed woman. You're causing a draught in here. Can't you do nothing right?' he said, as he spat into the fire.

We went outside and the back garden was a mess. 'Gary, this is the dog. He was a German shepherd but he's old now.'

I knelt down and the dog could barely lift its tail up and I opened my palm, and offered him my biscuit, hoping to get a reaction but he looked at me as if to say, leave me alone.

We went back inside, and Helen handed me a pile of comics that were all sticking to each other. As I browsed and peeled my way through old copies of *The Victor* and *The Bunty*, I watched the hands go round on the grandfather clock that was sitting in the corner and I listened to it ticking until it was five o'clock and I could leave.

Mum and I met at the end of our street, and I didn't tell her how much I hated going to that house. I went there every day after school and after a couple of months, Mum told me that I couldn't go back to that house as Dad's auntie had a mental breakdown and she had to go into hospital.

There was nowhere to go but where I wanted to go in the first place. As I walked up the road from school with my key hanging around my neck on a piece of string, I was excited at the thought of being alone in my house, watching *Scooby-Doo* in the dark and eating a sandwich of margarine and Heinz brown sauce.

It must have only been a few weeks later and I was watching TV when I heard blood-curdling screaming noises outside. As I walked to the window, the hairs on the back of my neck stood up. I pulled apart the white net curtains and grey daylight squeezed in through the gap, and I saw a procession of people all dressed in black and white. They were hugging each other, and the women all had black veils over their heads. The men had their heads down and they were carrying a tiny wooden coffin, which was covered in white, black and red flowers. A big horse and cart was waiting and I saw my mum walking along the street. Then a woman started wailing and moaning, and she was speaking in a language I had never heard before. Mum tried to walk across the street to see her, but two men stopped her. The wailing woman fell to the ground as the men laid the coffin down and pushed it on the back of the horse's cart, and another woman threw a black sheet over the wailing woman.

I ran to the door and Mum was there. 'That was terrible there son. Do you remember meeting the woman in the street when we first moved here? Her boy couldn't get the toilet?'

I nodded but I could only remember the wee boy with the old man face. 'Yes, I remember her mum.' '

Well Gary, that's wee Patsy gone with the angels now.'

I had never seen this before and I asked Mum, 'Is that what happens when we die? Do we get taken away by a horse?' Mum told me that they were Roma gypsies, and this was a tradition that they had been doing for hundreds of years.

That night, I had a nightmare about Mum lying in a red coffin and I was trying to fight my way through the bushes to get to her as she was being taken away by a black horse. Dad was dressed like a priest, and he was carrying a big cross and he was praying. As the horse and cart moved away, I woke up sobbing and I was relieved it was morning. I jumped up and ran to the top of the stairs and shouted,

'Mum, are you there?' Mum shouted up, 'Where do you think I was?'

It was the weekend again and we got on the bus and walked down the road as usual. As we walked past the pub, I noticed there was a convoy of trucks and caravans driving across the mud and the forgotten islands of grass. Each year, the carnival and the carnival people would arrive and invade this wasteland, setting up their trucks like a fortress, and they would then unleash their mechanical dinosaurs so people could ride on them for a pretty penny. They would entice people in with loud popular tunes from through the years and dress up their rusty facades with colourful neon light bulbs and paint. As we walked, a caravan's wheels bumped over the pavement, splashing into the mud. Mum told me she had worked with the carnivals a long time ago and she told me to stay well away from them, as they were trouble. I was puzzled, and as I shrugged my shoulders we arrived at Dad's front door.

The next morning, I woke up and Dad wasn't there. I knew the story as I had heard it so many times, so I didn't ask. I went outside to play in the 'backies' and I could hear thunder rumbling in the distance. The sky was grey, and the red clouds were crushing the blue ones in a violent overture. I went exploring and found a burn and there were tadpoles dashing about in the green moss. I followed it downstream, hoping to find some frogs to play with. I played outside until the black clouds rushed in, and the rain came teeming down and I ran through the wet bushes to get back to Mum.

We had our dinner, and Mum washed the dishes while I got ready for bed so I could watch my favourite program, *The Six Million Dollar Man*. We both sat down and heard the words, 'Steve Austin, better, stronger, faster', and I was glued to the telly. Just as Steve finished beating up another evil bad guy until the next week, there was a tapping on the glass of the front door. Mum got up to answer the door, she reached the lobby, and stopped while looking along the dark hallway that led to the door. As it creaked open, she turned on the light, and said, 'Bert, what the hell is that?' I could hear my dad say, 'It's a monkey.'

I jumped off the settee and went to join Mum. I looked down the hall and Dad was carrying a monkey. Mum was smiling as she said, 'I know it's a monkey, but where did you get it? Look at the state you're in. What have you been up to?'

As Dad stood there cuddling it, I looked at his face and his cheekbones were bruised, and his knuckles were torn and bleeding. I thought it might have been the monkey and then I looked at his vest and I saw he had spilt tomato sauce on it again.

Dad lowered the baby chimpanzee down and it walked towards me. It was wearing a red T-shirt and jeans and was chattering its teeth and clapping its hands as it walked to me. I put my hand out and it gently held my fingers with its rough, hairy hand and we walked to the settee. It jumped up and sat there staring at me and I stared back. As I looked at it, I thought about Tarzan, and I wondered where the chimpanzee's mum was and why he wasn't in the jungle. Mum and Dad came into the living room, and I listened to my dad tell his story.

'I was playing cards with the travellers up the road. I met them in the pub, and they were playing for money, so I went along. We played for a couple of hours, and I was on a winning streak. There was a bit of money on the table and I had a good hand. Not a great hand, but I was in for a penny, in for a pound and there was no going back. Long story short, the pikey lost the hand and he owed me money for the hand I won. He was going mental, and I was surrounded with all these travellers. He told me he couldn't pay me and him and his pals got together and told me to fuck off and that they had a deal for me. Annie, the next minute, a gypsy woman walks in holding the monkey and I knew then he was the deal. I asked him what the deal was and the pikey said he wanted to fight me for the monkey. I was surrounded but I told them I would fight him for the monkey and the money on the table. I had no choice and I had to fight him, as I wasn't leaving without the money.

Mum said, 'Bert, they could have killed you. What were you thinking?'

As I was listening to Dad, the chimp came closer and

stood up next to me, sinking into the cushions on the couch, and it looked at me with big glassy eyes and I put my arms around his jeans and felt his spongy nappy, as he sat next to me.

Dad laughed and said, 'I know, I thought I was a goner. Anyway, we walked outside, fought in the mud, and I won the monkey and the money, and here we are.'

Mum got up off the chair and laughed and said, 'Do you want a cup of tea? Where are you going to keep him? A monkey in Dundee!'

Dad replied, 'I don't want the monkey. I'll sell him. He can sleep with me tonight and I'll get rid of him tomorrow.'

That night, I couldn't stop thinking about him. Dad told me he was going to take him somewhere that would get him back to the jungle. I shared the bed with my mum and as I tossed and turned, I imagined the chimp running and swinging through the trees, and into Tarzan's arms, just like on the TV. The next morning, Dad and the monkey were gone.

Although we had moved, Mum still kept up her friendship with Mabel and a few other women and we always looked forward to going back to see them and the children that played in the street. Mum would drink tea and chat about old times, and I would play tig, chickenelly, cribie and marbles and when we had to leave to catch the bus,

I always looked up at our old tenement's window, wishing we could just walk up the steps and into the closie with the broken light. It was always hard leaving but, as I sat on the bus, I knew I would be seeing them again and Mum always told me I had to make new pals wherever I went, as in life, people would come and go and that's just the way it was.

Since moving, I had made one pal and his name was Tommy We met in the gym hall, which also doubled as a place where they served the school dinners. We were all sitting there, waiting, and watching these old hags, bulging out of white aprons, and their hair was up and every strand was covered by a white net. As they pushed the trolleys past us, the smell was revolting and suddenly, we all wanted our mums to be there, but reality kicked in when the wheels on the cart stopped at our table.

With a big spoon, and a hand that looked like it was made of sausages, there were comforting words of, 'Hurry up. Geez yer plate … I've no got all day … eat this and you'll get pudding, and if you don't, yer getting nothing.'

The woman wiped the sweat from her neck and wiped it on her belly. I looked at the boy across from me and he looked as bad as I felt, and I asked the woman, 'What is that?' She grabbed my plate and said, 'Boiled liver and gravy with dough boys.' I looked at her in horror as the liver pieces floated in the brown water and were clinging to the dough and, as the smell wafted up my nose, I started to dry retch and then the whole table followed. As the boiled offal was plated up, the boy sitting across from me thought he would go one better and as he pushed his chair out from the table, he vomited then fell backwards onto the wooden floor.

The woman and the cart moved on and I helped the boy up and said, 'My name's Gary. What the fuck was that?' The boy wiped his mouth and replied, 'Em no eating that shite! I'm Tommy.'

We became close pals and Tommy started to come down to my dad's house with us at the weekends and sometimes he would stay over and get picked up the next day.

It was a warm, humid day and the sun was out, and we were making the most of it, out playing in the backies, and I decided to take Tommy on an adventure down the burn. In the past, I had only gone so far and stopped, as I was on my own. As we made our way through the bushes the branches were scratching our arms and we were covered in midges bites, but we kept going. We pushed our way through the thick nettles that were growing out of the creek and as we broke and ripped the dead twigs off the maze in front of us, we came across a flat piece of ground that had cardboard boxes and old blankets and filthy sheets hanging from a big tree like a tent. To us, it was like a den and a secret hideaway. As we got closer, the cardboard box moved and suddenly a man appeared, and he was holding his private bit in his hand, and it was big and pointing up the way. He said, 'Come here boys, do you want a sweetie?' as he began pulling on his willie. I was in front, and I knew Tommy was behind me as I could smell his breath and the cheese and onion crisps he had eaten before we left. As I stepped backwards through the burn, Tommy was standing, and he was frozen with fear. 'Tommy, move back. Move! We need to get away from him.'

The man was smiling, and he made a run towards us, but we were smaller, and we managed to fit through the hole in the bushes to the other side. As we ran, we didn't look back, nor did we stop until we reached the top of the hill. We were panting and looking at each other. Tommy was shaking. I said, 'Don't tell yer mum as she won't let you come back to play with me. C'mon, let's get a drink and a biscuit.' Tommy said he wouldn't tell his mum, but he did, and he stopped coming with us at the weekends after that.

I didn't go exploring as much anymore and I watched the TV, drew, coloured in, and heard Mum and Dad argue and fight. I would hear the noises of struggle and the sounds of domestic turmoil going on in the kitchen. I was trapped in this place, but I would go to another space in my head. It was a place of my imagination, filled with colours and pictures that I would put down on paper.

The screaming was loud again, as I was jolted back into my dad's living room. I sighed as I put down my pencil and pushed myself off my knees as the noises became louder. I was nervous and had to make myself go through the door as I felt I had to, but I didn't want to see what was coming next. Dad's voice was drowning out Mum's and as I turned into the kitchen, I heard the smacking of Mum's skin. Mum fell on the floor, and Dad dragged her along the ripped linoleum until he saw me standing in his shadow. He released Mum and he brushed past me and swiped his jacket off the chair then left. I ran over and cuddled into Mum's back as she was bent over and sobbing. She was sitting like a puppet with the strings cut off and her knees were bleeding. When she raised her head to look at me, all I saw was sadness through black mascara tears. We packed our bags and walked the walk up the road, as the sound of the carnival raged.

They say time heals and I watched Mum's face go from red to black to blue. I tried to understand what I had seen, and I wondered if this was what everyone did when they were in love.

I remember his smile, and when he laughed his eyes could light up a room, and when they laughed together, in my mind the room became smaller as I watched them. But most of all I remember seeing his intense stare of madness and rage.

My mum was a no-nonsense, straight-talking woman who had a big heart. Although she was hard, kindness was her greatest asset. Was it just that they shouldn't have been together? Or did they meet each other at the wrong time in their lives? Or maybe they lived on broken promises.

Whatever it was, even though I was only a boy of eight, I knew this couldn't be love.

Just as Mum healed, Dad would come back, and I would be told they were getting back together, and it was as if nothing had happened. I would hear Mum pray that things would be better for us and, as I listened, I wondered if she was trying to convince God or herself.

It was a couple of weeks later and we were back at Dad's house, and I was playing hide-and-seek with the children from the scheme. I heard Mum shouting on me, and I looked up from my hiding spot to see her waving for me to come in.

'Geordie, I have to go, my mum wants me. See you next time,' and I ran down through the long grass and over the timber fence.

Mum was standing at the back door and the light was shining on her face and there were tinges of yellow bruising on her cheek as she smiled and rubbed my hair. 'Gary, your dad is home, and he has something he wants to show you in the living room.'

I walked in and saw my dad standing by the window holding a big dog and when it saw me it barked and I jumped. Dad said, 'Son, it's okay, he is friendly. He won't bite. He's a boxer and his name is Caesar and he's yours.'

The dog barked and he stood up and started wagging his tail end. I stepped closer and my dad let go of the rope and I put out my hand and patted his hard head and rubbed his velvety ears. Mum appeared and she was smiling and said, 'You've wanted a dog for a while now and here he is.'

The dog jumped up and licked my face and there was saliva all over his slobbering chops and mine, and I didn't care. I was laughing and spitting at the same time, and I couldn't remember being so happy. My mum and dad walked out of the living room and I sat on the settee admiring my new pal, Caesar. He was brown all over with white patches on his chest and around his ears and his coat felt smooth yet spiky. As I lay down, he jumped up and pressed himself into me and he laid his head down and stared at me as I dozed off wondering what I was going to feed him and where he was going to sleep.

Mum came into the room and woke me up and said, 'Right, c'mon Gary, we need to get going. School tomorrow.'

I jumped up and stretched my arms and back and Caesar was pouncing around the living room. 'C'mon boy, we're going home.'

Mum was packing her bag and said to me, 'We can't take him with us. He has to stay here with your dad so he can look after him. We will see him next week.'

I started to cry. 'No Mum. We can look after him. He needs to be with me, and I need to be with him.'

As she was putting her coat on, she said, 'Caesar has to stay here and that's the end of it. C'mon, get your bag. We need to go.'

I put my toy gun and soldiers into my bag and put my

anorak on and I spoke to Caesar and cuddled and kissed him as he sat looking at me.

Mum said, 'C'mon, we will see him soon'. As we were leaving, I ran back and hugged his thick neck and I squeezed him tight, not wanting to let him go. Walking up the road, I knew I would see him soon, and I counted the days until I did. As the months went by, we were inseparable, and wherever I went, he was with me.

I was upstairs and heard Mum talking to Dad. I walked to the top of the stairs and sat down so I could hear what they were saying. Mum was pleading with him and there was a panic in her voice, that I had never heard before so I knew something was wrong. I crept down the stairs and listened. 'Bert, that is wrong. You can't do this. He loves that dog. It's all he has. Please Bert, don't sell him. I'm begging you.'

I started shaking and it is hard to explain what emotions were running through my body all at once. I was overcome with nerves, and I could hear my heart beating fast in my head and I couldn't breathe. As I fought back the tears, I gulped a lump in my throat and I could hear a sizzle noise inside, and my heart was aching. I buried my head in Caesar's ears and he knew something was wrong and he didn't move, and he licked my face until I stopped crying.

All I heard was Mum crying and begging him not to take Caesar away, and all Dad said was, 'I'll get him another one.

He'll get over it. I'm out of here and when I get back, I'll tell him.'

I sat on the stair and my jumper was soaked with bitter tears and I decided that he wasn't taking my dog and we would run away. I waited until the shouting stopped and I heard him leaving and I crept down to the kitchen and Mum wasn't there. I saw her outside, hanging out a big basket of washing, and I knew this was my chance. I ran upstairs and grabbed my bag and came down to the kitchen and made a whole loaf of bread, butter and strawberry jam sandwiches and put them back in the plastic bag. I looked out the window and the basket was still half full. I put my coat and beanie on and slung my schoolbag over my body. I grabbed the long rope and threaded it through Caesar's collar, walked out the front door, through the rusty steel gate, and didn't look back.

As I wrapped the rope around the arm of my duffel coat, I spoke to my dog and he answered me the only way he could, by pulling me further and further away. 'Caesar. We need to go. He was going to sell you and take you away. I don't know where I'm going boy, but we'll be okay. Fuck! Did you see the size of that truck?'

As we walked, big articulated trucks were whizzing by us, splashing and spraying the roads with waves of water. I wasn't scared and I continued talking to him. 'Hey boy, lucky they missed us. We would have been soaked. Are you hungry? We'll get a sandwich in a minute.'

We kept walking and the sky was going black and it was getting darker by the second. Misty smirrie rain started to fall, and it was blowing across the yellow lights on each side of the road. The truck and car lights were beaming and, in the distance, I saw a sign saying M90. I walked and wondered where we were, and it was pitch black and cold. As we got closer to the motorway, I saw the shape of a big shed and the door was open and there was a barbed wire fence around it. I pulled Caesar over as he stopped and didn't want to move. I looked around the fence and a bit had been cut. As the rain battered down on us, I pushed Caesar through and I jumped through the gap. We tiptoed inside the dark space of the shed, hoping there wasn't anyone inside, pulling on their willie.

We sat down on a pile of old timber that was stacked along the corrugated iron wall and as I looked out the double doors of the rusty shed, the rain was hammering down as the lights of the cars flashed by. The old tin roof was in bits. I reached in my bag and took out the jam sandwiches and we had one each, then another and Caesar took a liking to them and stuck his nose in the bag and ate them all. 'Caesar. What are you doing? That's all we have boy. They had to last us.' We lay back and I made a pillow with my bag and Caesar snuggled into me and we fell asleep.

I don't know how long we were sleeping but a truck blasted its horn and it made us jump and I started thinking about my mum. I looked at my dog and he stared at me.

I said, 'Do you think we should go back? Mum will be worried. Dad will realise how much I love you and not take you away. You ate all our sandwiches, and I don't know where to go.'

Caesar looked at me as if he understood what I was saying and I said, 'C'mon boy, let's go back.'

I followed the road back and the rain had stopped. As I turned the corner into my dad's street, there were flashing lights and beams from torches going back and forth in the darkness of the long grass. I saw the neighbours as I got closer and Mum saw me and ran towards me shouting, 'Gary, thank God you're okay! Where have you been? I was worried sick and the whole street has been out looking for you.'

As soon as I was in her arms, I started to cry and said, 'I'm sorry Mum. I run away as I heard him say he was taking Caesar. Tell him Mum. Tell him not to take him away.' Mum cuddled me and didn't say anything. We walked across the road and down towards my dad's house. The police came over and asked if I was alright and they told me it was a silly thing to run away like that. We walked down the street and through the gate and Dad was standing there in the darkness of the doorway.

At first, there was silence and then as Mum walked me into the living room, Dad grabbed my wrist and he dragged me to the stairs and the more I tried to resist, the harder he pulled on my arm. I was grabbing anything I could but it was futile. When we got to the bottom of the stairs, he pushed me down, face first, and he stepped on my back to get over me. He heaved me up the long stairs to the top, and said, 'Get in that fucking room!'

I replied, 'You're not taking Caesar! Don't take him from me … don't take him away!'

Dad stared at me with a crazed look I had seen before and he began kicking and punching me in a frenzy. I instinctively curled up into a ball and as the thuds reigned down on my back, my thoughts were with Caesar and the pain of losing him was far greater than my dad's blows.

Eventually, he stopped and as I twisted my head to look at him, he looked exhausted, and his wet hair had fallen forward and there were sweat trails running down his face. I looked at him as he turned away and said, 'You're not taking Caesar,' and he pulled the door closed and locked it. I brought my knees up to my chin and I buried my face into my rain-soaked jacket and cried, and I knew I would never see my dog again.

Mum and I left the same night and as we walked, we didn't speak a word to each other. What was there to say? When we got home, I ran up to my room and Mum spoke to my sister in the kitchen. I sat on the stair landing and they were whispering, but as I got closer, I heard every word.

'Mum, you need to leave him.'

'Pat, it's not as easy as that. He is Gary's dad. If it was, I would have done it years ago.'

My sister said angrily, 'That 'B' is putting you and Gary through hell, and you keep going back to him ... Why Mum?'

'I don't know what to do Pat.'

They walked into the living room, and I crept upstairs, and their words were muffled as I emptied my bag on the bed and wondered where Caesar was.

Mum was still spending too much time around the toilet bowl and the mince and stew got the blame again. She was working in the factory and was still putting in nights at my auntie Cath's pub. I had nowhere to go so I had to go with her. As Mum pulled pints, I watched the black-and-white TV with the fuzzy picture in the 'back shop' and I would draw and transport myself into a world of colour until it was time to go home.

It was a dark and smoky, run down, piss-and-beer-spilt dump and it had every character under the sun drinking there. The wallpaper was woodchip and there was linoleum laid throughout. There were stools along the bar where the regulars sat, drinking half pints and nips of OVD rum or whisky from morning till the last bell. It was like there was a changing of the guard as one 'alkie' would leave, staggering out, and another would take the stool for his session. The pub was located in the middle of Dundee's booming jute mills, and as soon as the men and women working there received their little orange envelopes for their slave trade

thrall, they would all teem through the swinging doors of
The Scouringburn to freedom and intoxication.

My auntie would flick the switch and the cracked and
broken walls would come alive with light and sounds of
the 'puggy machine' – the jukebox – and at weekends, there
was a disco that had five coloured bulbs, and a mirror ball
hanging by a piece of fishing wire. The music was loud and
there were orange, green, yellow and red lights flashing over
the black canvas of the dance floor, and there were sparkles
of silver stars, shooting from the tin foil ball in the ceiling.
The women stood facing each other, with their handbags in
a pile at their feet, as 'little Jimmy Osmond' serenaded them
with his song, 'Long Haired Lover From Liverpool'.

There was a pool room in the back and as Mum cleaned up
at closing time, I was allowed to go through and hit the white
ball around the table. Sometimes I would wait until Mum
and Auntie Cath had their backs turned then slip under the
bar to sneak through to the pool room. The room was filled
with a smoky haze, and it had four custard-coloured walls.
Years of spilt beer and dampness were masked by umpteen
coats of paint and the linoleum floor was ripped from years
of abuse. There were three chairs at one end and a pool cue
rack that had a cube of blue chalk swinging from it.

One night there were four men in the room and one of
them said, 'Hi son, does your mum know you are in here?'

When I replied yes, he said, 'Right son, come over here
and grab a seat and watch me beat this prick.'

The other man chalked the end of his cue and said, 'Fuck off. Are you playing or talking shite or what?' The men laughed and I smiled.

I was watching their every move until I saw Mum standing in the doorway. She wasn't happy and she had her arms folded and said to me, 'Get through to the back shop now. I told you not to come through here.' The man took his shot and looked over to Mum and said, 'Ach Annie, he's okay here with us. We will look after him.'

Mum answered, 'Gary, get your arse over here now. And you, shut yer puss, or I'll throw you out. I don't want him in here.'

As I ducked under Mum's elbow, she hit me over the back of the head and as I left the room, the men burst out laughing.

Mum sat me down and said, 'I told you I didn't want you going through there. It's rough in there. They play for money and sometimes there is trouble and people get hurt. There are a few hard nuts in there. Do you understand son?'

Mum turned and walked out then she spun around and threw me a packet of crisps and said, 'Sit there and don't move.'

I had used up all my paper drawing and there was nothing on the TV, so I repositioned my chair and watched the lights and the women dancing. All of a sudden, a man came staggering onto the dance floor. He had a big gash across the top of his head and blood was spurting out like a fountain. The women stepped back and screamed and raised their hands as if to say stay away. The man was walking like the Frankenstein monster and then another man ran around, facing him, and he was carrying a pool cue and he whacked the stick over the man's already injured head. The man collapsed to the floor and the other man threw the broken stick to the side and ran out the door into the night.

Auntie Cath rang the bell that hung above the bar and Mum told everyone to leave. The ambulance arrived and they took the injured man away on a stretcher. The police came and then another ambulance arrived, and they carried another man out on a stretcher and the two paramedics carried through a younger man and sat him down on one of the chairs from the pool room. As he removed the shirt from his face, I could see a deep, hideous wound that ripped across his cheek and nose, down through his mouth. It was the men from the pool room and my mum was right.

After everyone left, my auntie and Mum sat at the bar and had a drink and as I drank my Coke, I listened to their every word. 'What a night Annie!'

My mum sipped her drink and said, 'What a night alright. That young laddie will be scarred for life over a game of pool. He's a cheeky bugger but he didn't deserve that Cath.'

'No Annie, he didn't. C'mon, let's get cleaned up so we can get home.'

I watched them swig back their drinks and they both cleaned up the puddle of blood on the dance floor and

Mum left my auntie Cath to go and clean the pool room. I followed her through, and I stopped at the door and stared at the walls and the floor; there was broken glass and blood splattered everywhere.

Mum appeared from the toilet carrying a mop and she poured Vim and disinfectant into the bucket and swirled it around then she brushed up all the glass and said to me, 'You see son, that's why you can't be sneaking through here, you hear me? What If you were there tonight?'

I agreed and nodded my head. 'Mum, did you see that man's face? Did he get punched?'

Mum was on her knees, wiping the blood streaks off the skirting boards and walls. 'Gary, that wasn't a punch, that young lad was tumblered, which means he was hit by a glass across his face. From now on, you stay in that back shop.'

I picked up the pool cue and sank the white ball in the top pocket and said, 'Okay Mum.'

It was 1973 and I was in my room and my sister had on the song 'Love Train' and I was trying to dance like the men from the pub. I was getting ready to go to my first disco and I didn't know what to expect.

I walked down the road to the school, and I waited in line with the other people from the schemes. The teachers were there watching, to make sure everyone paid in, and we were given a stub that was pulled off a big roll. As we pushed open the heavy fire doors and headed into the dark, the music hit our ears and it was magic. I bought a plastic cup of cola and as I stood and watched everyone dancing, I was so happy to be there.

Saturday and Sunday had been and gone and as I was eating my Monday morning cornflakes and milk, Mum told me I had to meet her at the factory as Dad wanted to see us. I didn't want to go but I had no choice.

I went to school and they told me to get a haircut, then I tackled the school dinner with Tommy, and I jumped over a horizontal pole and landed on a big spongy mat in gym class, then it was time to leave and walk the long walk to meet my mum.

I sat on the chair and looked through the big window, wondering if I would see any naked women, and then Mum came through the swinging door, and she smiled when she saw me. 'We need to go and meet your dad up the Perth road. We need to get on two buses, so I'll buy you a sweetie for the journey.'

We walked to the bus shelter and there was a strong wind blowing as we waited for our bus. We shuffled on and took our seat. I looked out the window and watched the trees being bent over by the force of nature. I ate my chocolate bar and Mum talked to a woman she knew from St Mary's.

We got into the town centre, got off the bus and onto another and the rain started to fall. As we stepped off the bus, I could see my dad walking through a small car park and he was standing under cover as the heavens opened. Mum and I ran up the hill and when we reached my dad, I noticed there was no embrace between them.

He was soaking wet and his slap-back hair had collapsed. As he stood under the light of the building, there were shadows that made his face look like a skull, and I watched his face change back as he moved and the shadows left him.

Mum shook herself and said, 'Terrible night to be out. What did you want to see us here for?'

Dad replied, 'Annie, we need to take Gary for blood tests. I need to know if he is my son.'

Mum grabbed my shoulder and she put her warm hands over my cold ears and said, 'What are you talking about! What the fuck are you playing at Bert? He is your son! He is your spit. Look at him! Gary is your son and there's no need for any tests.'

Dad stared intensely at my mum and said, 'I need to know he is my son. C'mon Gary, come with me,' and he tried to grab my coat, but Mum pulled me backwards, and she said, 'Fuck off Bert, you're not hurting me or Gary anymore.'

She grabbed my hand and walked out into the rain and Dad shouted, 'Don't walk away from me. You'll be sorry. I'll get the blood tests one way or the other.'

'Leave us alone!' Mum shouted as we walked down to the bus stop.

As we stood in the rain, it was bouncing off the oncoming

cars and the black tarmac was shiny with white and yellow lights. Way up the road, we could see our bus home.

We got on the bus and there wasn't much to say so we just looked out the window at the people getting soaked. When we got off, I said, 'Can we get a bag of chips?' and Mum said, 'C'mon, let's go to the Deep Sea and we can sit in.'

I looked at the sorrow in Mum's face and we ordered fish and chips, and Mum got a pot of tea, and I got a bottle of Coke with a straw. We sat at the window until we dried off, and looked out through the faded net curtains. Outside, it looked like it was the end of the world.

My teacher was writing on the blackboard and I was looking out the window. As I glanced over, I saw my dad's head through the small square window in the door. He was making a face and I could read his lips saying, 'Come outside.' The children were all looking at the door and the teacher turned around to explain what she had been writing on the blackboard and she noticed Dad. She nervously put down her chalk, walked to the door and went outside to talk to the stranger. The whole class was staring at the teacher's head nodding and talking and then the door opened, and she called my name. 'Gary, your dad is here, and he wants to talk to you. Go and see him. Right children, these are our times tables …' and that is all I heard.

As I left my desk, I walked to the door, and the room and everything in it was blocked out and I was on my own.

He was standing there smiling and he was dressed in his usual dress jacket and pants with an open-necked white shirt, and his hair was perfect. 'Gary, we need to go away for a while, and we need to be brave and get these tests done.'

I answered him, 'No! Mum said no tests. Where's my mum?' and I started to cry.

Dad started to panic, and his voice changed, saying, 'Do you want to stop seeing me and not have a dad? They will stop us seeing each other. Do you want that?'

I was nervous and confused and I didn't know what to say, and as I cried, I said no, and he said, 'C'mon then, let's go.'

We walked past the walls plastered with children's drawings with their names on them. When we reached the door, Dad pushed the bar down and it flew open hard as the wind caught it, and we walked down the steps to the playground. Dad's car was parked across from the open school gates, and he had left the doors unlocked.

I watched his every move, and he turned on a cassette and Johnny Cash was singing about a boy with a girl's name.

We drove for a while and then pulled into the side of the road and Dad said, 'Wait here, I won't be long. I have to pick up something here first, then we are going to see a woman I know. '

I listened to a song about a ragged old flag and the beats

of the drums stayed with me. My dad came back as the song ended and he was carrying a plastic bag. He threw it in the back seat and I asked him if he could play the flag song again. We listened to the song, and he told me where we were going.

'Gary, we are going to see a woman I know. Her name is Avril, and she is a good woman, and we will be staying with her for a while.'

'Where is my mum? I want to go home.'

His voice changed again, and he said, 'You can't go home just now. Your mum is okay, and we need to stay with Avril just now. I don't want you crying, do you hear me. We are nearly there so you better be good.'

There was a parking spot across from a pub that had boards on the doors and windows and barbed wire along the top of the roof. Next door was a row of derelict shops. Dad reversed into the space, and said, 'I'm warning you. No crying in front of Avril.'

We jumped out of his car and walked up the council tenements' path and into the 'closie'. The smell of piss and shite hit my nose and somewhere a big dog was barking. The woman lived on the bottom flat and as we got to the door, I noticed that there was splintered, sharp wood all the way down to the concrete and the pale blue paint on the door had scratches of white and was blistered all over.

Dad knocked on the door and I could hear the woman humming as she opened her front door. I looked up and saw a woman with blonde bubble hair, and I was amazed how high it was sitting without falling over. The next thing I noticed was her chest, as it was sticking out like the woman in the factory's. She wasn't naked but she was almost there. As she bent over, her two breasts spilled out, and she said, 'Hello darlin'. You look just like your dad. Look at those shoulders! With muscles like your dad's, you could be a soldier one day.'

As I looked at her, I pictured in my mind's eye a soldier running down the street, stopping at the corner, and aiming his gun at the shop windows.

'My name is Avril. Come inside. The fire is on. Hello Bert.'

I walked into her small living room and as I turned around, I saw my dad kiss the woman with the wasp's nest haircut and I wished I hadn't.

They came into the room and Dad handed me the bag from the car and he said, 'Son, it's for you. A present. Open it.'

The woman leaned into him and tilted her head and said, 'Aww, Bert, that's lovely.' I took the brown-papered box out of the plastic bag and ripped the tape off to reveal a picture on the box of a man with a ripped, disfigured face. I took the wrapping off and read 'The Abominable Dr Phibes' and I said, 'Who is he? His face looks like the man in the pub that was hit with the glass.'

Dad looked puzzled then said, 'He's a monster from a

film years ago. I know you like horror films so I thought you would like him.'

I opened the box carefully and pulled out the figure. The woman and Dad shuffled backwards, and Dad said, 'Son, you play with your new toy. I have to go in the room and talk to Avril about something. Watch TV and we will be out soon.'

I didn't say anything, and I looked at the monster's face and thought about the scars on the man in the pub. As I kneeled on the carpet, the woman was making noises and the room got darker and darker.

A few days had gone by, and I missed my mum, but I was too scared to say anything or cry in front of the woman. I watched the TV, and my dad had a lot to talk about in the room with the woman called Avril. Dr Phibes wasn't much fun to play with on his own, but I had plans for him as soon as I was allowed to go home.

The next day, we were eating breakfast and Dad and Avril were talking about taking me to the clinic once we were finished. The table was next to the window that looked out to the street and the shops across the road. As we ate our toast, a police car drove up and down the street slowly and I thought they were lost.

Dad saw the police, and as they stopped outside Avril's tenement, he jumped up and said, 'Avril, I need to go and see a man about a dog.' I said excitedly, 'A dog!' and Dad said, 'Not that kind of dog. C'mon, Gary, let's go. Hurry up. I'll call you later about the clinic.'

We walked towards the front door and there was a knock on the door and a woman's voice behind the door, saying, 'It's the police.' Dad grabbed my arm and looked at Avril and said, 'It's the police. We are not here.'

Avril said, 'What the hell are the police doing here Bert? What have you done? I don't need any more trouble and you have brought the police to my door. Well you can fuck off.'

She brushed past Dad and answered the door and when she saw the policewoman standing there, she said, 'Bert, don't call me again. He's all yours boys.'

The policewoman told me to come with her and I grabbed my new toy and the box, I put it in the plastic bag, and we walked out of the 'closie' and into the back of the police car. She asked me if I was okay, and she wanted to know all about Dr Phibes. Not long after, the policeman jumped in the front and he turned and smiled to the woman and me, and he drove me home to be with my mum again.

Mum was standing at the front gate as the police car pulled in. She had been crying and she had her hand over her mouth as the policewoman helped me out. 'There's your mum son. Go and give her a cuddle.'

I ran to her and wrapped my arms around her, and she said, 'I'm glad you're home. Are you hungry? I'll make you something. I'm sorry son. I was worried sick as I didn't know where you were.' Her face started to contort and as she cried, I felt her pain through the top of my head.

I looked up at Mum's distraught face and said, 'Don't cry mum. I missed you and I'm glad to be home.'

The policeman rubbed my mum's shoulder as they spoke and I ran off to the bushes to find my Action Man and introduce him to Dr Phibes.

This would happen another four times. Dad would either get me while I was walking to school, or he would be waiting at the school gates and each time he would trick me into getting into his car or van and there was always another Avril waiting, with big dangly earrings and big hair and painted eyes. But after all was said and done, he never did get my blood.

The police would come and go, and my mum's life of agony was slowly taking its toll on her. He was killing her softly and he was never going to let her go. As time went on, Mum sat me down to tell me that she was going back to him and this time, things would be different.

I had missed so much of school that when I sat in the classroom, it was like the teacher was talking in another language, and I would look out the window and daydream about Caesar, the bear, and the monkey and where they were.

SUFFERING IN SILENCE

It was a bright sunny morning as I said cheerio to my mum. I walked down the road and as I saw the school's black fence and the white church next door, I thought about sitting in that classroom trying to understand what the teacher was writing and then I thought about not sitting in the classroom and that sounded better, so I walked across the busy road and past the church and before I knew it, I was walking around the grocery store, filling my face with chocolate biscuits and crisps and drinking milk from the carton as I walked up and down the aisles.

I hadn't planned to go anywhere and, as I left, I took two packets of Fruit Club biscuits and stuffed them inside my duffel coat. I stepped out of the shop and into the street, turned around and no-one was there. The scheme was dead and deserted and I watched the children from the other schools running and playing in the playground then I lay on the grass and ate a Fruit Club biscuit, and I watched brilliant blue skies, and the white clouds turned into dogs and dragons as the wind pushed them away.

In the distance, I could see trees, so I followed the road until I came to the start of the forest. There was a yellow sawdust path and a sign hanging crooked on a fence saying, 'Templeton Woods, no cars or motorbikes'. As I took my first step, it was soft and spongy, and after a while, the yellow path turned black, and every step made a crunching sound as my feet broke the branches into twigs. There was no sun in the forest and there were birds making noises as they protected their nests, high up in the blackness. I came to a road, and it had a stone wall following it, and I followed the wall until the darkness crept in.

I had explored enough for one day and when I got back to the edge of the forest, I ran as fast as I could, as my imagination got the better of me.

The next morning, Mum was upstairs getting herself ready for work and I saw her bag sitting on the settee and it was open. I looked inside and her purse was poking out. I picked it up and shook it about and the purse jingled with coins. I opened the zip and there were brown coins and a few silver ones, so I took a few of each and pulled the zip closed. I heard Mum's feet as the timber moved under the carpet and as she came into the living room, she said,

'C'mon Gary. Another day. Let's go. I'm running late. Did I pull that plug out?'

Mum checked the plug was out and the ashtrays were cool, and we left. 'See you tonight. Be good and watch the roads.'

Mum walked along the street and I waited until she turned the corner and I made my way to the bus stop. I stood in the shelter trying my best to not look like I was guilty of anything as, in my mind, getting on the bus on my own was a crime. The bus pulled in and I paid the fare and ran up the tight, winding stairs and sat at the window. I counted the coins in my hand and, as we moved, I watched the buildings and houses fly by.

The bus was packed, and people were standing and holding on as the bus bounced and sped down the road into town, and all of a sudden, the whole bus stood up, and we were there. I followed everyone off and they all went in different directions and then it was just me.

I walked past the shops, and I bought a packet of sweeties and looked in every shop window. I found a toy shop and stayed there until the man told me to leave. I had nowhere else to go, so I walked back to get the bus home and, as I sat at the window, I thought about Tommy playing in the playground on his own.

That night, Mum was biting her nails and she was quiet and the TV was off. We had our dinner then we went to bed early. As I lay in my bed, the light was streaming in my window, and I could hear children playing out in the street.

The next morning Mum said I had to go down to my dad's house after school and she would meet me there. I went to school and I played with a tennis ball with Tommy and we ate fish fingers and Angel Delight from the woman with the big belly, and I looked out the classroom window until it was time to go.

On the way to my dad's house, I played at a park made of concrete and people must have thought the park was a toilet as there was shite and puddles of piss inside the coloured-graffiti-sprayed rooms and tunnels.

I walked past the pub and I reached his house. I knocked on the glass window and I could see his figure and white string vest coming towards me. The door opened and he said, 'Get your coat off and go and sit in the living room until yer mum gets here. I'll be upstairs.'

There was an atmosphere of quiet dread in the room, and as I sat on the settee, I counted the flowers on the wallpaper until I saw Mum walking through the gate.

Dad closed the living room door and began talking to Mum outside. I heard my name getting mentioned and as soon as I heard the words purse and stealing, I knew I was in trouble, so I moved off the settee and went behind it.

The door opened and Mum and Dad walked in. Mum had a strained look on her face and Dad was smiling as he spoke. 'What are you hiding behind the couch for? Come here, I want to talk to you.'

Mum said, 'Bert, don't hurt him. I want you to talk to him, that's all. I know he won't do it again.'

As he stared at me, the room got smaller but this time, not in a good way. I was trapped and there was no escaping this.

Mum's voice changed with a more urgent tone, and she said, 'Don't hurt him,' and Dad said, 'I know he won't do it again, as he will remember this day. Gary, get over here now!'

My legs and hands were shaking and all I could say was, 'No! So you can batter me? Mum, tell him not to batter me! Please Mum, I'm sorry Mum.'

As I was looking at Mum, he rushed me and grabbed my arm and pulled me over the back of the settee. I sat on the edge of the cushions, waiting for what was to come.

Dad looked at me and said in a calm voice, 'Now tell me the truth. Did you steal money out yer mum's purse?'

He then took my wrist in his hand and held it tight, and as he took my four fingers in his other hand, he said, 'Did you take money from yer mum's purse? If you don't tell me the truth, I will break your fingers. Tell me the fucking truth.'

Mum started to plead with him, saying, 'Bert, he's your son. Don't do this! He is sorry'

As I cried and told him I was sorry and begged him not

to hurt me my dad looked me in the face, and he bent my fingers back as far as they could go. I screamed in agonising pain and Mum jumped on his back and she was screaming and swearing at him to stop, but he kept going.

The torture continued, the room went black, and all I remember was waking up on the settee with my mum cradling me and wiping my forehead with a cold face cloth.

He was gone, and Mum walked me up the stairs to the bedroom, put me in bed, and tucked the covers in tight. I was drifting between consciousness, sleep and thoughts of what had just happened, and as my mum left the room, I held my toy gun in my hand and I wished it was real.

We didn't go to the hospital and the life we knew carried on.

One day, Mum was cleaning and dusting, and she had all the windows open and the crisp breeze was whirling through the house. The phone rang and Mum took a draw of her cigarette and stubbed it into the black Cutty Sark ashtray that was sitting on the mantelpiece. She was on the phone for a few seconds then hung up and said, 'Gary, I need to go out for a wee while. Yer Granny has had one of her falls again and I need to go and pick her up from the hospital. I won't be long.'

Mum left and I vacuumed the carpets while I thought about Granny and where she had been. We didn't see much of Granny until my mum or Auntie Cath got the call to come and pick her up from the police station or the infirmary.

I would hear Mum talking to her sisters, reminiscing about their mum, saying that when my grandad was alive, they were inseparable and they had a deep love for each other, and when he died, she just couldn't cope as she missed him so much and she started drinking. She never had any money, and anything she had went on the booze.

I can remember one Christmas, she wrapped up an orange for me and put it under the tree, and Mum said that it was the thought that counts.

She started off on the whisky, then the cheap wine, and eventually, she would drink anything she could get.

She was a feisty, small Irish woman who always wore a hat, and she carried a tiny tin with her that had snuff in it, and she would sit and inhale the powder up her nose. There would be snuff stains down the front of her cardigan and a trail of black crust around her nostrils and her top lip. She had a funny smell that clung to her but whenever she came to stay with us, she always made me laugh.

There was a tap at the door and I knew it was my mum. I unhooked the two chains, opened the door and saw her standing with my granny. 'Gary, hiya son. It's yer auld granny here again. Look how big you've got, and those eyes are getting bluer every time I see you. Give yer granny a cuddle.'

I put my arms out and noticed her dress was stained and

wet and there were stains of blood on her white blouse and cardigan. As I cuddled her, I could feel how frail she was, and she smelt of piss and beer.

Mum was standing behind and she said, C'mon son, let's get inside. C'mon, in we go,' as she supported Granny's arm. 'Watch the step Ma, I think you've had enough falls already.'

Granny answered, 'Ach shoosh you. Have you got any whisky?'

I moved to the side and smiled as Mum ushered her through the living room door. 'Ma, you've had enough drink. You need to get a cup of tea in you and something to eat. That's the only drink you'll be getting here.'

Granny sat down on Mum's chair, and she mumbled, 'Fuck off Annie, I need a drink.'

Peter Pan was on the TV and as I watched my granny stare at Tinker Bell prancing about, I looked at her broken face, and there were blue coloured stitches sticking out like lions whiskers on her eyes and chin, and a wet patch appearing on the cushion where she sat. She had drifted off to her own world of neverland.

The longer she stayed with us, the more stories she told me. She would talk about witches and her 'old country', and tell me ghost stories and tales from when she was a wee lassie, and how hard it was. She would talk about her eight children, but she never ever mentioned my grandad's name.

One of her more memorable stories was when my mum

was making dinner and as she sat there on Mum's chair, she said, 'Son, this is a story from a long time ago, and a different world to what we live in now. It was dark outside and there was a big storm coming in and my mother was lying in her bed dying and everyone had come around to see her for the last time as she was leaving this world for another. My mother was a witch and ...'

I was wide eyed and couldn't believe it, and I said, 'A witch!' and Granny said, 'Yes, she was a witch, and she had the gift of the second sight. She loved your mum, and she made a doll for her out of cloth and sticks and your mum took this doll everywhere. There was a line of people waiting to say their last words to her and she kept saying, "I want to see Annie".

'More people came, and my mother said to me, "Send these people away, I want to see Annie."

'Your mum was about your age, and she was kneeling on the floor beside the fire, playing with the doll, and I told your mum to hurry up as her granny wanted to see her before she passed. I grabbed her arm, and we ran through to the room where my mother was lying, but it was too late. She died and the room was very cold, so I took your mum back to the fireplace and when we got there, the doll was burning in the fire.'

'Fuck! Sorry Granny. How did it get in the fire? That's scary.'

Mum came through with my granny's dinner and said,

'What's scary?' and I said, 'Your doll in the fire.' Mum shrugged it off and made a face, saying, 'Is that you trying to scare him Ma? Gary, go and get the salt for your Granny.'

As time went by, Granny became angrier at Mum. I would hear her say, 'Annie, one drink … just one,' and Mum would say no, and Granny replied with, 'I'm your mother and I want a drink. It's like living in a fucking jail here.'

She stayed with us for as long as she could bear it, and I watched her soft pale face heal as she stared out the window every day, and her bones and every bit of her cried out for a drink.

One day, my granny left without saying anything and she died not long after, and I didn't get to go to her funeral.

It was a Friday night, and we packed our bags and got on the bus as usual. We made nervous small talk as we walked past the pub and little did we know that this would be the last walk down this road to my dad's house.

It was my ninth birthday and Mum made dinner and we had chocolate and stayed up late and watched Muhammad Ali knock out George Foreman in the jungle. After the fight was finished, I stood between Dad's knees, and it would be the last time I felt my dad's muscles.

The next day, Mum and Dad were in the kitchen and the shouting started and I was cracking up inside. I sat on the floor, holding my hands over my ears with my eyes squeezed tight saying to myself, 'Stop … fucking stop.'

The shouting turned to screaming and I felt myself shaking. I stopped drawing and jumped up and opened the living room door. As I turned into the kitchen, my dad had Mum's hair in his fist and I shouted, 'Stop! Stop you fucking bastard. Leave her alone.'

It did the trick and he looked at me and brushed off my mum like he was swatting a fly. His face changed to venom, and as he moved, I moved quicker. He chased me into the living room, and as I jumped through the bottom window, his hand swiped thin air, and I ran around the side of the house and jumped over the wooden fence and through the jaggy nettles. When I reached the top of the hill, my heart was beating that fast I could hear it thumping in my head. I climbed up a tree and wedged myself in between its limbs and waited until it was dark.

As I walked back, I resigned myself that I was going to get battered and hoped he had saved all his strength for me and not my mum. When I reached the back door, I climbed up the drainpipe and onto a small roof and I stood there and banged my fist on the window ledge until the hook bounced off its cradle. I dug my fingers into the putty around the window and pulled the frame out, and when the window opened, I dived through headfirst and tumbled onto the wooden floorboards below.

The room was filled with junk and old furniture Dad had

bought and there were dust-ingrained white sheets covering antiquities of shite scattered around the corners of the room.

I moved over to the door and opened it and took the key out. The hallway was dark and silent. I closed the spare room door and turned the key and made a bed out of the mouldy, embroidered cushions that were piled up on an old chair. The stench of dampness, rotting wood, and Dad's Old Spice aftershave lived in the walls.

Darkness engulfed the room and as I got comfy and my senses got used to the smell, there was a tap at the door. I jumped up as I knew it was my mum. It was too quiet to be him.

She whispered, 'Gary, are you okay? Your dad left and I don't know when he will be back. Are you hungry?'

'Are you alright Mum? I'm not hungry and I'm staying here.'

'Son, we have to stay here tonight but in the morning we are leaving and we are never coming back here. I'll see you tomorrow. If you hear anything, stay there, don't come out, do you hear me?'

I said, 'See you tomorrow Mum,' and I went back to the cushions.

I lay back and I looked out the big window and thought about fish fingers, chips and beans, and I saw puffy white clouds moving and I watched the shape of the moon as I drifted off to sleep.

The next day, light streamed through the space where

curtains should have been and as I rubbed my eyes, I realised that there was no noise and I had slept through. I got up, crept to the door and walked down the stairs where I saw our two bags sitting at the sink in the kitchen. Mum appeared and told me to put my coat on and we left.

We left his house, and I left the 'backies', the burn, the big tree I used to climb, the children in the street, and I left that horrible room with the shadows and the smell of his house. But there were some things that just couldn't be left behind.

The weeks went by and life went on and it was quiet and peaceful. Mum worked and worked and cleaned, and she drank her Carlsberg Special Brew and, as usual, she used every ashtray in the house. She would make her homemade soups and stews, and the coughing and the acid bile was always there, and she played and sang along to her Shirley Bassey records as she dusted her toby jugs. Every night, she prayed for us.

I went to school, and I couldn't catch up and I looked out the window and played with the tennis ball. I ate their school dinners, and I was told I broke a few school records for throwing a steel ball further than anyone else, and for jumping over a pole onto a bouncy mat and the teacher told me I had to get a haircut again.

Most of the time, I would go to my world of colour and imagination. I went there even more when Tommy told me he was leaving and he couldn't play with me anymore as he was going to a place called South Africa. When he did leave, he was like my granny, and he left without saying goodbye.

My sister had moved out and she got engaged so I didn't see much of her, but she called my mum every day. I came home from school and as I dumped my bag on the floor, I noticed Mum was home and she was on the phone to her. I heard my mum say, 'Pat, it's over. It's been four weeks and I've not heard from him, and I don't want to … No! I'm not going back to him. He has hurt us enough so don't worry, I'm not going back to him … Pat, I'm never going back … Okay Patricia Ann, I'll see you tomorrow. Goodnight.'

I was just about to walk through, and I saw my mum sit in her chair and close her eyes and pray. I had only heard her pray at night. I sat at the bottom of the stairs and listened as she said, 'Please God, keep us safe. Keep him safe. I have made mistakes in my life, but he hasn't. I am tired of this life, and I know I need to keep going for him, but can you just give me a sign that things will get better. Thanks. Amen.'

I opened the front door and closed it again, and shouted, 'Hi Mum. What are you doing home?' Mum said, 'I got away from work as I wasn't feeling too good. I'm alright. It must have been that mince from last night.'

Later that night, Mum sat on her chair, and she had a couple of drinks, and we shared a bar of chocolate as we watched the TV. As usual, I lay down and stretched out on the settee that was directly below a big window that was furnished with net and velveteen curtains. The Friday night horror film was coming on and Mum read the paper as the film started. The living room was dark and the only light that was on was the small table lamp in the corner, beside the mantelpiece and my mum's chair.

I loved horror films and I loved the characters and the monsters. I had magazines of Lon Chaney, Bela Lugosi and Vincent Price up in my room. *Jack The Ripper* was on and he was following a buxom young woman down a cobbled street in old London town. He was dressed in black, and he had a top hat on, and he was graceful but menacing as he held the butcher's knife in his hand.

I was engrossed in the film as Jack was getting closer to the terrified woman, and my mum looked up from her newspaper and said, 'I'm going to make some supper. Do you want a bit of cheese on toast as it's Friday night?'

I didn't look at Mum as the woman had run down the dark, wet street, and as I stared at the TV, I said, 'Thanks Mum. I think this woman is in trouble now.'

The light went on in the kitchen and Jack had the woman cornered and begging for her life. On the screen, all I saw was his black figure, walking towards the woman.

Mum shouted, 'It's ready, do you want pepper on it?' and the woman screamed a terrible scream that I recognised and as she raised her hands up to her face, and Jack raised his arm up, showing the shining blade, there was a huge crashing noise in our living room.

In a split second, there were thousands of splinters of glass all over me and tiny icicles of glass were everywhere. I lay there stiff, and I was in shock and terrified.

I saw Mum stop at the kitchen doorway and she screamed 'Gary! Are you okay? Don't move. Please God … Fuck … Don't move.'

I stared at the TV and Jack was making a mess of his own and I said, 'Mum, don't come in here. The glass will go through your feet.'

Mum walked towards me and I slowly sat up. The glass was sticking to my flannelette pyjamas and it was in my hair. 'I told you not to move,' said Mum. 'Stay there. Listen to me.'

I stood up and tried to shake myself and there was glass flying about like fairy dust. I watched as Mum walked through the pain to get over to me.

'Gary, are you cut? Are you bleeding anywhere? Don't move.' And I said, 'I'm okay. I'm not cut.'

'Thank God, you're alright … Thank God … Son, lift up your arms so I can get your top off.'

I lifted my arms up to the side then up further and I watched Mum grimace in pain, as she peeled my pyjama top off and there were fragments of glass sticking into her fingers.

As we stood there, we looked out the void that used to be our window, and a crowd appeared, dressed in house coats, and they were watching us and pointing like we were animals in a zoo. Outside, I could see the yellow glow from the streetlights, and then they were drowned out by blue and red flashing lights. As I looked across our living room, the lights were dancing around the walls and the settee. The carpet was glistening with sparkling icy shards and my mum's hands were covered in blood.

The door knocked and Mum shouted, 'Wait a minute.'

I said, 'Stop Mum. It's the police at the door. They are here to help us. I won't move. Go and get the door.'

My pyjama top was covered with Mum's blood, and as she walked away to answer the door, I took off my bottoms and used them to stand on. I looked out to the street and one of the neighbours pointed at me as I stood in my undies. The police car's lights were bouncing off the tenements walls like it was a school disco.

There were two policemen and as they walked into the living room, they looked at me standing there, shaking and shivering in my underpants, and one of them said, 'Are you okay son?' I said, 'I'm alright. My mum's fingers are bleeding, and she needs help.' The other policeman replied, 'We'll look after your mum.'

They walked towards my mum, and she met them at the kitchen door. One of the policemen said, 'Do you have any idea who would want to do this to you?'

Mum was looking down at her hand, trying to pick out needles of glass that were sticking in her fingers. 'I think I know who did this.'

The policeman said bluntly, 'Who?' and Mum said, 'It was Gary's dad … It was him. I know it was, he's fucking nuts.'

The policeman looked at his pal and made a face then said, 'Does he live here? Why would he do this? Are you separated?'

There was blood dripping on the carpet and my mum walked into the kitchen to get a cloth, and she said, 'He doesn't live with us, he has his own house, and I left him four or five weeks ago. I couldn't take any more. He's a fucking lunatic.'

The policeman then said, 'Did you see him do it?' and my mum shook her head and said, 'No, I didn't see him do it, I was in the kitchen making toast for me and Gary. He could have killed my boy.'

My mum's face changed, and I knew she was trying not to cry, and there was pain and desperation in her voice as the policeman said, 'Okay, we will talk to him.'

Mum put her head down and lifted up her hands to show the police her injured fingers, and said, 'Talk to him? What good will that do? Look at the fucking state of us! Look at my boy. For fuck's sake, help us. For God's sake.'

The policeman reached out to my mum, and she stepped back and pulled her bleeding hands away, and he said, 'We can't do much unless we have a witness. Someone who saw this bastard do it. We can and will talk to him and we will ask him questions like where he was, and we can caution him, but at this stage, that's all we can do. I'm sorry.'

I was watching and listening to every word they were saying, and it was hopeless, and Mum said, 'My heart is breaking, and I don't know what to do. I just want him to leave us alone.' Mum sobbed and her soul seemed broken.

I walked over to the wall and there was a dent and a scuff mark on the corner of the wooden mantelpiece and I followed the scuff mark along the wooden furniture and when I came to the end, I looked down to Mum's chair and there was something embedded in it. I reached into the soft cushion and pulled out a piece of steel, similar to what I had thrown in gym class, and I took it over and handed it to my mum. The policemen and Mum looked at me and as she wiped away her tears, blood streaks were dripping off her chin. She gave the bloodied head of a ten-pound sledgehammer to the police, and I said, 'Mum, I found it over there. It was in the cushion on your chair, and it would have killed you if you weren't making me toast.'

The police left and we were on our own again. The neighbours had seen enough, and the disco was finished. The house was quiet, and Mum took me upstairs and put me in bed. Once again there wasn't much to say.

I closed my eyes and pretended to sleep, and she left me and went downstairs. I waited for a while then I followed Mum down the stairs. When I got to the bottom, the lamp was on and I saw my mum sitting in her chair looking at the window that wasn't there anymore, and in her right hand, she was holding a knife that 'Jack' would have killed for.

The next day, there were people everywhere. Mum managed to get every bit of glass out of the settee, but the carpet had to be ripped out, which meant more 'tick' to worry about. We got a new window, and the man gave me a big lump of putty to play with, and then we had to get ready to go to the pub.

'Gary, the taxi will be here in five minutes. Are you ready?'

Mum checked all the electricity was off and the ashtrays were cool and after one final scan of the room, she closed the front door and pushed it and shook it until she was happy it was secure, and we walked down the path and the taxi pulled up.

When we arrived at the pub, Mum spoke to Auntie Cath as they served the men on the stools and I fiddled with the coathanger aerial until the TV's picture stopped rolling. I was happy as my uncle Joe was coming to the pub and he always made me laugh and would give me a few coins out his pocket for sweeties.

I watched the TV until I heard his laugh as he came in the door and I jumped off the chair as he ducked under the bar and said, 'Gary, me boy! How's it going?'

'I'm good Uncle Joe.'

He raised his hands and pretended he wanted to fight me, and I did the same. He laughed and I hugged him, and he hugged me back. He smelt of beer and aftershave and a hint of women's perfume, and he was wearing a long coat with fur around the collar and was smoking a big cigar.

'Are you really okay son?' he said, as he looked in my eyes, and I said I was. 'Right, now I know you're okay, do you fancy a game of pool?'

My face lit up, then I remembered the man that looked like Dr Phibes, and said, 'Uncle Joe, my mum said I'm not allowed to go through there in case there is trouble.'

Uncle Joe winked, and said, 'Ach, You'll be alright in there as you're with your uncle Joe. C'mon, we can play doubles,' and he put his finger up to his mouth and ushered me under the bar. 'Hurry up now.'

The room was the same, but the walls were cleaner. There were four men in the room and there were two men at the table eyeing up their chances as they chalked their cues.

Uncle Joe smiled as he laid down his coin that staked his claim to play, and he said to me, When it's my turn, I'll beat these lads, and when I do, I'll ask them if they want to play doubles, and then it will be me and you against them.'

'I'm not very good.'

Uncle Joe smiled and winked and said, 'You're better than them.'

As we sat there, the atmosphere in the room had changed, and a man had just potted the black and the white at the same time and he threw his pool cue on the table and walked off in disgust, swearing as he left the room.

My uncle Joe was off the chair and smiling as he placed

the coin in, and he pushed hard until the balls rattled and fell. He took the balls and set them in order of spot, stripe inside the black plastic triangle and placed the white ball, ready to go. He stood back and chalked the cue and looked over at his opponent, and said, 'Heads or tails pal?'

The man said, 'Same rules and money as the last game ... Heads!'

Uncle Joe nodded then flicked the coin and it spun and bounced then landed on tails. The man said, 'Bastard ... On you go,' and Uncle Joe smashed the white ball into the triangle. The balls were going everywhere, and one of the striped coloured balls slammed into the pocket.

I looked at him walk halfway around the table, then chalk his cue, then walk the other way, and he stopped and took off his long coat and folded it and put it on the floor. He bent over and looked down the cue towards me and winked at me again, then proceeded to blast every ball into the pocket.

The man said, 'You're a fucking shark pal.'

'I'm no shark. You wanted to play for money. Does anyone want to play doubles?'

The man said, 'Okay, me and the shark against you two, how's that?'

Uncle Joe walked over to me and turned to the three men, and said, 'Thanks pal, but no thanks. I'm playing with my boy.'

The man laughed and said, 'Fuck off. Okay pal, have it

your way. Does anyone want to team up with me so we can beat the old man and the boy?'

A man put up his hand and stood up and joined him in the corner. 'Okay old man, do you want to up the ante. Let's make it interesting and give me a chance to get my money back.'

Uncle Joe put his arm around my shoulder and said, 'Ach, wait a minute, it's just a friendly game here lads.'

The man said, 'Are you fucking playing or what is it, are you scared?'

The atmosphere in the room had changed again and I was thinking my mum would be cleaning the walls again. Uncle Joe squeezed me hard and said, 'Okay, you know he's a wee boy, but I'll play your game. You set them up and we'll take tails.'

They threw down the money on the edge of the table and stepped back. The man flipped the coin and it landed on tails, and Uncle Joe said, 'Okay Gary, we are on. You break,' and I said, 'Me!' He made a face as if to say yes, now go and take the shot.

I was nervous as they were all looking at me and I lifted up the stick and I bridged the pool cue over my left hand, and I pushed with my right, and I hit the ball and it sliced off to the left of the cushion and it stopped moving without being close to hitting the triangle of balls and everyone laughed.

My uncle Joe came over and rubbed my head and said, 'C'mon pal, let him take it again.'

One of the men motioned with his cue giving the go ahead for me to try again, but the other man said, 'Fuck off. That's two shots for us. Have you got a problem with that you prick?'

Uncle Joe shrugged his shoulders and said, 'On you go.'

The man split the balls all over the table and one of the spotted balls went in the pocket. He smiled and chalked his cue and one by one the spotted balls disappeared. As he lined up the white ball for a good shot on the black, he said, 'There's only one shark in here tonight.'

The man took his shot, and it rattled the top pocket, but it would not fall. 'Fucking bastard. It's okay, he'll bottle it.'

Uncle Joe looked at the table, then me, and he cleaned up every ball. With only the black to go, he hit the white gently and the black ball rolled slowly up the table and fell over, into the pocket without hitting the sides.

The man wasn't happy and said, 'Fuck you, you prick,' and he threw the cue on the floor and walked out of the room. The other man came over to me and said, 'Well done wee man.'

My uncle Joe smiled, and he handed me a few pound notes. I couldn't believe it, and I said, 'Fuck!'

Uncle Joe laughed and said, 'You see son, there are sharks everywhere, so you will need to be a good swimmer like your uncle Joe. Now c'mon, we better get back before you get me in trouble.'

I stuffed the notes in my pocket, and as we walked into the dance floor, there was a good-looking woman, dancing with her pals. Uncle Joe smacked the woman on her arse and as she smiled, Uncle Joe said, 'Here, get yourself a drink.'

We ducked under the bar and into the back shop and it was like we never left. 'Right son, be good for your mum and remember, if you ever get caught doing something you shouldn't be, never admit to it, even if they catch you doing it, okay? Right, I need to go now as I need to see a man about a dog, so I'll see you later.'

As he left, I thought about what he said, and I thought about the money in my pocket but, most of all, I wondered who this man was that everyone wanted to see about a dog.

When we left the pub, it was raining, and we stood inside the swinging doors until we heard the peep of the taxi then frantically pulled on the cab's door and got inside. The driver had the heater on, and he was eating raw mushrooms out of a brown paper bag, and his name was Dave. He knew my mum and my auntie Cath, and he turned off the meter and chatted about everything and nothing. We said cheerio and got out, and the rain had stopped.

We walked up the path then suddenly Mum stopped and whispered to me, 'Gary, go and hide.' And I said, 'No Mum, I'm staying with you.'

It was after midnight, and it was pitch dark and there

was a black shape on the wall that was our front door, and it was wide open. I grabbed onto Mum's coat and we walked inside. We were quiet and the silence was terrifying as I expected my dad to be inside. As Mum felt around for the light switch, the lights didn't come on, and we moved slowly towards the kitchen.

I was wide-eyed as we got to the kitchen drawers and Mum took a knife and held it out in front of us. We crept up the stairs, and with every step, we waited for the unexpected. We went inside our bedrooms, and it was clear that someone had been and gone.

Mum phoned the police and told them that we needed help and she then took me next door to our neighbours, and we waited until the police came.

The police came and two men in suits talked to my mum. There was a social worker woman who had a notepad, and she was writing everything down as Mum spoke to her. There were two men in white suits, and they were dusting the furniture, and a man came and fixed the lock on our door.

The lights came on and as I looked around the living room, I could see that nothing was broken but all my mum's ornaments had been moved, and her toby jugs had all been turned upside down.

To live in fear was a terrible thing and when you lived in fear every day, and you tried to live a normal life, it was near impossible. And it was exhausting being scared of the light and the dark. I always thought my dad was just a whisper away, or around every corner, and in every 'closie' we walked past. He came into our house to scare us and to let us know how easy it was to get to us and it seemed like no-one cared and all we had was each other. While Mum prayed every night, all I had was the hope that he would leave us alone.

I had to meet my mum at the factory every day as she wouldn't let me go home. I was too scared to anyway, so I sat in the reception and looked through the big window until she came out.

We would get to the end of our street, and see a heap of gravel and stones dumped across our gate, and one day, we saw that the pile of shite was, in fact, a pile of shite. There was a truck delivery of manure and we had to dig our way through it to get inside our house.

A year had gone by, and it was my birthday. My mum and sister told me they were taking me into 'the town', and I met them at the factory so we could get the bus. We went to my favourite toy shop, and I was racing about the shop touching everything with enthusiasm. The thought that I could pick something new was giving me a feeling of joy and excitement I hadn't had for a long time.

The shop was closing, and I picked a red Indian figure that wore a buckskin costume. His name was Tonto and he was The Lone Ranger's pal. My sister bought me an Action Man and he was wearing a Royal Marines suit, and as we walked out of the shop, I couldn't stop looking at them.

We went to the Hong Kong Chinese restaurant and I looked at the big fish in the tanks and there were women dancing on the dance floor. We ate fried rice and chicken Maryland and picked out the crispy chips and covered them in curry sauce. The Chinese man brought us fried banana and ice cream, and we had an After Eight mint each at the end. We walked about the deserted streets for a while before we left my sister to get the bus home.

By the time we got home, it was time to go to bed. Mum came into my room and said, 'Hope you had a good birthday son. It's not every day you're ten.'

I pulled the covers up to my face and on one side I had Tonto and on the other I had the Commando Action Man and I said, 'It was the best birthday I've ever had Mum.'

'That's good. See you in the morning.'

Mum switched the light off and all I could hear downstairs, was the maniacal organ playing at the start of the program *World in Action*, and when he finished, I fell asleep.

I don't know what time it was when I was woken up by my mum's screaming and as I jumped up out of my bed, I could hear this massive banging and it wasn't stopping. The noise was reverberating around every wall and it was a continuous, bang, bang, bang. Mum appeared in the doorway, and she grabbed me and cuddled me in tight as she collapsed to the floor, at the top of the stairs.

Mum said in my ear, 'Stop. Please stop. Please God, get him to leave us alone.' As I held my hands over my ears, the banging stopped, and there was an eerie buzzing noise in the house, as if the house itself had stopped moving and we were the only ones shaking.

I looked at my mum's face and she had tears in her eyes, and I said to her, 'Is he going to kill us Mum?'

Mum straightened her back, took my arms and shook me, and said, 'Look at me! Don't you ever think like that.' And we both looked out the long window into the street and held each other until the shaking stopped.

The factory was a part of life for me now, and as time went on, the women that worked there would come out and say hello and give me chewing gum or a sweetie. I would sit there and look at the clock until Mum came through the door and we would walk up the road and we would keep going.

It was cold and the autumn leaves covered the factory car park, and there was a sea of red, brown and yellow leaves slowly dying on the streets and pavements as we walked up the road.

We were walking in the middle of the pathway when I heard the sound of a van, then it stopped but the engine was still running. I looked behind me and I knew it was his, and I said, 'Mum, he's here … He's come to get us.'

Mum turned around and he was running through the thick leaves towards us, and she stood in front of me and faced him. 'Gary get behind me and stay there.'

Dad got close enough for me to see that he had that same crazed look in his eyes that I had seen before, and he had a big butcher's knife in his hand. He was six feet away from my mum and he said, 'I'm gonna fucking kill you this time.'

Mum didn't move, and she shouted at him, 'Okay Bert, I've had enough, and I can't take this anymore,' and she ripped open her factory overalls and said, 'Here you are, you bastard. If you're gonna do it, fucking do it! Come on then … DO IT!'

He raised the knife above his head, and I screamed, 'NO! No Mum, no please!' as she stepped forward.

He looked down the road, then he stared at my mum and me. There was a group of women walking out of the factory car park and onto the pathway and they started shouting to us. Dad turned and ran away, and he jumped in his van then sped up the road and he was gone again.

The women gathered around us and asked if we were alright and my mum was stone-faced as she pushed her stud buttons back in and she said 'Thanks, me and Gary are fine.'

The women were all yapping and stating the obvious to Mum, and she nodded her head and said thanks, but as they walked away, we both knew the obvious wasn't that easy.

We walked through the leaves, Mum took my hand in

hers, and we didn't speak a word. We had our dinner and Mum said to me, 'I've called the police. I don't know what they will do this time, but when they get here, I want you to go upstairs to your room. I don't want them asking you any questions.' I tried to reply, saying, 'Why not? I ...' and Mum shouted, 'For once, will you just do what I tell you! Get upstairs now.'

I burst out crying and ran up to my room.

There was a knock on the door, and I left my room and waited at the top of the landing. As I peeked around the banister, Mum answered the door and there were two policemen and a woman dressed in a suit with a skirt.

Mum said, 'C'mon in. Thanks for coming.'

As they went into the living room, I went down the stairs with Tonto to listen. Mum told them what happened and when she finished, the police said nothing, and the woman in the suit said, 'Where is Gary?' And my mum answered her, saying, 'Gary is up in his room lying down.'

The woman said, 'Has he eaten?'

My mum replied, 'What? Yes, of course we have eaten. Do you want a description of what we had? What the hell is this? What kind of question is that? I've just told you, that bastard came at us with a butcher's knife in the street and you're asking me if I have fed my son?'

The woman said, 'Can I see him?' and Mum told her, 'No, I told you, he is tired, and he is lying down, and I don't want him answering your questions. He's been through enough.'

I bumped down to the bottom of the stairs and looked through the door and Mum was sitting on the edge of her chair, looking over at the settee.

The woman said, 'Are you still with this man? You know this isn't good for your son to see this and I am here to assess this situation. It has been going on too long. You have a daughter, yes?'

I could see Mum sitting there, totally demoralised, and she answered the woman by saying, 'Were you not listening to me? I am not with Gary's dad and I haven't been for a while, but he won't leave me alone and I need help and that's why I called the police. What situation? What are you talking about? I don't want to be with him. He's a lunatic, and he has been torturing us for a long time and all I hear from you lot is that you can't do anything.'

The woman ignored what Mum said, and she replied with, 'Where is your daughter and does she see her father?'

My mum put her head down and looked at the carpet and said, 'My daughter is out a lot with her pals, and she has a boyfriend, so she isn't here much. Gary's dad isn't my daughter's dad. What assessment? What the fuck are you here for?'

The woman's voice changed, and she told Mum, 'There is no need for the bad language. I am here to assess if Gary is in a safe environment and I have to tell you that from what I have heard tonight and what you have told the police, and also looking at the history of this case, at this stage, I am leaning towards removing Gary from this situation.'

My heart sank as Mum's head dropped further into her chest. My stomach was in knots and there was a fizzing in my throat and an ache in my chest as I tried to swallow and understand what I was hearing from the woman in the suit.

Mum pushed herself off the arms of the chair and she said quietly, 'I want you to leave now. This bastard is after us, and all you can say is you're taking my boy from me. He is all I have. You need to go.'

They made a move and all I heard as I went up the stairs was 'We'll be in touch.' As I watched them leave, I saw my mum close the front door and put the chains on the hooks and she rested her head on the door and she cried for a long time.

After they left and I heard the sound of the TV, I came downstairs to see Mum. She was in the kitchen and when she saw me, she put her arms out wide and said, 'My boy,' and I squeezed her as tight as I had ever done.

I cuddled her for ages, and she said, 'Go and get your pyjamas on and we'll watch the late film. Who's on tonight?' and I answered, '*The Wolf Man*' and Mum laughed.

We watched the film together and Mum said, 'What a load of shite! But you like it so ... Right, c'mon, bed! Get those teeth brushed or you'll end up with teeth like Lon Chaney.'

I jumped off the settee and said, 'I'll wait for you Mum,'

and Mum said, 'Get up those stairs and into bed. I'll be up in a minute.'

Mum went into the kitchen, and I left to go up the stairs. I heard Mum flick the switches off around the living room and the bottom of the stairs went dark. As I reached the landing, I rubbed my eyes and looked out the long window. The street was dead and empty and the lights on the poles were sending a yellow glow into the tenements. And then I saw a car stop at the end of the street and I saw a figure getting out, and it was him.

He started to run towards our house, and he was carrying a brick in his hand, and I stood there, frozen with fear, as I knew what was coming next. All I could do was think of where my mum was, and as I screamed a hopeless scream, I pissed all over my pyjamas and the warm sensation flowed down my legs onto the carpet.

I screamed, 'Mum! Mum!' then there was the familiar crashing noise of shattered glass, and I ran as fast as I could down the stairs to find my mum.

'Mum!' There was no answer and as I got to the living room, Mum was kneeling on the carpet in the dark and I kneeled beside her and hugged her desperately and said, 'Mum, are you okay?'

She couldn't speak but I knew her body wasn't hurt, and she was sobbing, and Mum mumbled, 'Just leave us alone.' We sat in the dark and didn't move until the living room was a disco again.

As the living room shimmered and sparkled, there were the men in white suits, dusting again, and there were two policemen, and two men in suits, talking to Mum.

Mum was sick of the questions as she'd heard them all before, and as I sat on the bottom step, smelling of piss, Mum answered the man in the suit, saying, 'I keep telling you the same things. You need to lock him up.'

The other man in the suit replied, 'And we keep telling you the same things. If you don't have a witness or someone who saw him, there isn't much we can do. We know he is a lunatic, and we know it's him, and we know from talking to him that it's him but we can't get him on anything as it won't stick unless someone saw him.'

Mum's face changed again, and her eyes filled up as she spoke with the voice of a broken heart, and said quietly, 'I think he is going to kill us.'

I stood up and my wet pyjamas were sticking to my legs, and I looked at the two men and said, 'I saw him. It was my dad. I stood up there on the landing and I watched him throw a brick through our window.'

After a while, the police left, and they said they would be in touch.

Mum cleaned and cleaned and no matter how much she vacuumed, the piss and the glass from that night was ingrained in the carpets.

We kept going, and Mum went to work, and I went to school.

The police said they needed time to collate everything they had, and until they did, they said they would talk to him. They explained to us that we would need to go to court, and I would need to stand up and talk. My mum was against me going to court, but we didn't have a choice.

Not long after, I was playing with a ball in the playground and there were children running about everywhere. Behind the school gates, I saw my dad, sitting in his van looking at me. When I saw him, I looked back at him, then I ran deeper into the playground where the girls were skipping and playing elastics. At night as I lay in my bed, I watched the shadows playing tricks on me, and I would squeeze my eyes open and sit up in my bed, staring at the walls until they left me.

It was the morning of the court, and my mum was crying, and I heard her talking to the neighbour and she said, 'Mary, I don't want him going to court. He's just a wee laddie and he shouldn't be put through this and it's my fault.'

Mary said, 'Annie, you and Gary don't have a choice in this. Bert is fucking nuts and you need to get shot of him. If you don't, he will keep coming back, and look, this is your chance for a new start for both of you.'

I stuck my head around the corner and said, 'Hi Mary. C'mon Mum, we need to hurry up.'

We got in the taxi, and we were let out at this huge

sandstone building. We were taken through a secret tunnel that led us into a brightly lit room that had four chairs and a big desk that had coffee cup ring stains on it. The room had a blackboard that was white on the wall.

We sat down and no-one talked, and a policeman came in and offered my mum and sister a cup of tea. There was a woman who talked to my mum outside and she came back in and sat there with her legs crossed, chewing a pencil.

The police detectives arrived, and they told Mum I had go with them and the woman, as they had to talk to me. Mum and Pat started crying as I left, and the tea policeman said to me, 'Be brave son.'

They sat me down and they took turns telling me what to do. 'Son, there is going to be a man questioning you when you get inside the court. He will be trying to catch you out and make you slip up. He works for your dad, and he will do anything to get your dad off. Do you understand?'

I nodded and said, 'I understand, and I will tell the truth.' I couldn't have been very convincing, as the two detectives had the look of concern on their chubby faces, but I knew what I had to do, and I didn't need anyone telling me. I had seen my mum hurt enough and I didn't want to see it anymore.

As we sat there waiting, the tea policeman stuck his head between the wall and the door, and he said, 'You're up in five minutes.'

The detective said to his pal, 'This will be the only chance to get this bastard,' and his pal said, 'Yeah, I hope the wee man is okay up there. Right Gary, are you alright? Your dad will be in the next room, so don't look at him, okay?' I nodded, and he said, 'Let's go.'

We stood up and I followed them up the small steps and everyone was staring at me. There were two long tables that no-one was sitting at and there was a smaller table and sitting there, smiling, was my dad. He was dressed as I remembered him, and his hair was slicked back and as he looked over at me, I stared back. There was a dead calmness in me as I focused my eyes on him while I sat there waiting.

The lawyer stood up and spoke to the crowd and the judge, and he said, 'My client is an upstanding citizen of this city and through the years he has been involved in a host of charitable events. I will prove to you today that he has done nothing wrong and that this is a spiteful case of a woman not being able to accept that the relationship with my client was over. I will prove that this woman has indeed had it in for my client for years and ...'

The judge butted in and said, 'You're going over old ground. Do you have anything for this young man?'

I didn't realise he was speaking about me until he looked over.

Dad's lawyer smiled a smarmy smile, and his teeth were like the cat from *Alice in Wonderland*. His cheeks wobbled when he spoke, and he said, 'Hello Gary. How old are you?' And I replied, 'Ten.'

He then asked me what time I went to bed, and I said, 'Nine,' and he showed me his teeth and said, 'So, we have established that on the night your mother's window was broken, the police arrived at 1.30 am in the morning, so if we can work our way back, what time were you going to bed?'

I knew where he was going with the question and I said, 'It was after *The Wolf Man* film, so it was about twelve.'

I watched him move around the table and he said, 'That's rather late for a ten-year-old wee boy now isn't it?' And I said, 'No, I like watching the horror film on Friday night.'

Dad's lawyer looked around the room and said, 'I will tell you what happened on the night in question. You were tired and you had just watched a scary film and your eyes wanted to go to sleep. You wanted to stay up past nine o'clock and as you walked up the stairs to bed, you were probably exhausted and rubbing your eyes. You had heard your mother talking about your father earlier, and she poisoned you against him. You have gone off to bed with this in your mind and when you looked out the window, the truth is, you didn't see your father did you? This could have been anyone, and you chose to believe this. How could you be sure of anything? Tell me Gary, you didn't see anyone, did you? Tell everyone the truth so we can all go home.'

I looked at him and then I looked over at my dad, and said, 'It was him. It was my dad. I saw him put a brick through my mum's window and I watched him run away.

It was him. I know how he runs, as I've seen him do it often enough.'

There was cheering in the room, and the policeman took me out and the detectives were happy, and my mum and my sister were crying outside as they waited on me. They all said I was brave, but I couldn't understand what all the fuss was about. I was just glad it was over.

Mum and Pat took me to a shop and they bought me a red satin bomber jacket that had three white stars on the back. We went for our dinner at The Deep Sea and we had fish and chips.

My dad was gone but so was my innocence and naivety. I was a ten-year-old wee boy, but I was no longer a child, and my life was altered forever.

I left my gun somewhere in the bushes and didn't go back for it. My toy soldiers became casualties and were lost in the mud, and I retired my battle worn Action Men and put them in a box under my bed. Dr Phibes came to a sad ending as I watched him get taken away by the bin man, but I couldn't let Tonto go, and he stayed with me for a long time after.

We moved on and we kept going. I don't think my mum got over it; or maybe, she just couldn't get over him.

FROM DESPAIR TO WHERE

When we got home, the atmosphere in our house had changed and the rooms seemed different and that bit brighter to me. Mum was still working hard as ever, and even though she would work all day and come home and go out at night, I think working in that pub was her sanctuary, as she would laugh and chat to the characters on the stools and the girls from the jute mills, and this helped her heal. She was still having a drink and a smoke as she cleaned and polished, and as always, she would sing her songs as she made her homemade soup. She didn't have to look over her shoulder anymore or be scared, but she still prayed every night for God to look after us anyway.

'Please God, give me the strength I need to keep going, and watch over us as we go. Take him somewhere, where he will be safe in life.'

Although my dad was gone, he was still with me lingering about somewhere in my head and he wouldn't leave.

We were in the kitchen and Mum was making our dinner. She was shaking the chip pan and a plume of steam flew up and the boiling fat sizzled and she said, 'Gary, I want to talk to you about something.'

'What's wrong?'

As Mum shook the golden fries in the basket, she said, 'Nothing's wrong, we have a chance of a new place for us. A new start for us. It's in the 'multis'.'

'I know where it is Mum. I thought you liked it here and you just bought new carpets again and we've got good neighbours.'

'I know, but this new place has a shared washroom at the bottom with a tumble dryer and everything we need, and I know a woman who lives there, and she said it was safe. Pat will be getting married soon and it will just be me and you.'

I said okay and we walked into the living room with our TV dinner, and she said, 'Okay, we will need to go up and see it next week. It's a new start for us son.'

I didn't care where we lived as long as she was happy.

When the day came, I stood at the bottom of this huge concrete building, and as I looked up I could see thousands of windows and wet stains on the grey walls. There were black birds flying in and out of the gaps, their nests sitting precariously in the corners of the roofs.

Mum shouted on me, and I ran into the foyer, and she was so excited to show me the laundry room. As we walked in, the noise of tumbling washing and small machines vibrating and bouncing about the concrete floor was deafening. There was a woman folding some clothes and Mum said hello to her and she then told me what each machine did and where the tokens went in.

We left the room and my ears were ringing. Mum pressed the button and the lift door opened and we walked inside. I had never been in a lift before and as it moved, I heard the cables strain and heave us up and then it stopped, and we got out at level fifteen.

There was a smell of piss as we walked to a door that had the letter B on it and as Mum turned the key, I knew this was going to be our new home. It was a small, two-bedroom, council flat that had a tiny kitchen with big fold-out windows and views on both sides.

Mum said, 'What do you think? This will be alright for us. Did you see that washroom? And there's only one door to worry about so we'll be safe here.'

And I said, 'Good Mum, what bedroom do you want?'

We moved in a load of boxes and the removal men tried their best to fit big squares into round holes and some furniture didn't make it into the lift.

As we made the last trip back to St Mary's, Mum and I

checked we hadn't left anything behind. As we stood in the empty living room, we looked out the big window to the tenements and we both said nothing for a long time.

Not long after we moved in, it was my sister's twenty-first birthday and on the day, Mum was busy making corned beef, egg and tomato, meat paste, and spam sandwiches, and there were boxes of crisps and packets of nuts piled up in the kitchen, ready to go. Mum was at her happiest when she was making food for people and as she took a swig of her Carlsberg lager, she would sing in her best Shirley Bassey voice, 'Mem'ries, like the corners of my mind, misty water-coloured memories, of the way we were' and she would bring the house down as the song finished.

The party was going great, and the disco was belting out 'Don't Go Breaking My Heart' and everyone was up dancing. I had brought a pal from St Mary's with me, and we walked around, eating sandwiches and crisps, and we had sips of all the drinks that were sitting on the tables, and after a while, we felt a bit funny.

Near the end of the night, an argument had broken out between one of my aunties and her sister, and I grabbed a few sandwiches and told my pal to get under the table. As we sat there, it was like watching from a ringside seat as Mum's two sisters punched and scratched their way out of the church hall and into the street. There were glasses smashed and chairs and tables knocked over and a whole lot of hair pulling and shouting until my mum and Auntie Cath stepped in.

With everyone gone, me and my pal helped clean up the mess and we looked around in case anyone had dropped any coins from their pockets. As I looked over, I saw Mum make a face as if she was in pain, and she was holding her side as she talked to Auntie Cath. She then continued picking up the chairs that had been knocked over and I didn't think any more about it.

We got a taxi home and as we stepped into the lift, the floor was sailing in piss, and we had to stand on our tiptoes as we were transported up the shaft to our landing.

A few weeks later I was running towards the playground gates and I stopped as I saw my sister standing outside and she was waving at me. I wondered why she was waiting for me and as I approached her, I said to her, 'Hi Pat, what are you doing here?' She told me that Mum had been taken to the hospital and she was here to pick me up so we could go up and see her.

'Is Mum alright? She was fine this morning when we left the house. What's wrong with her?'

'They didn't say much but when we get there, we will find out more. C'mon, let's go.'

When we arrived and we walked into the hospital the smell of disinfectant and the heat in the corridors was making me feel sick. As we walked, I looked into the rooms, and the further we walked, it seemed like the people were getting more sick looking.

We got to the ward and my sister spoke with the doctor and I slipped through the curtains that had been drawn and saw my mum lying in bed and she was sleeping. I followed the tube that was sticking from her arm, and it was attached to a bag, and there was another tube coming from under the white bed covers, and there were yellow and brown stains all over Mum's hospital gown. I sat on the chair and stared at her and tried to listen to what the doctor was telling Pat.

My sister came through the curtain and as she held her hand over her mouth, she said, 'Mum has an ulcer and they think it has burst inside her and it's making her sick.'

'What's an ulcer, and why is mum a funny colour? Is mum going to be okay?'

Pat told me that an ulcer could be caused by worrying too much and she finished by saying, 'Mum will be okay. Don't worry … C'mon, the doctors said we need to go now.'

We left Mum and walked back to catch the bus and I thought about the ulcer inside her.

The next time we went up to see Mum, I was sitting on the chair at the bed, and she slowly opened her eyes. There were a lot more stains on the bed and her gown, and she looked worse than before. As Mum lay there, she was taking shallow breaths and she said, 'How are you son?' and I said, 'I'm okay. How are you feeling? I heard about the ulcer.'

My mum strained a smile and said, 'I'm not too good but they tell me I'm in the best place.'

My heart sank and I had this overwhelming feeling of fear and dread and Mum said, 'Do you remember Ann? Ann McVicar?' And I said, 'Yes, she was your pal from our first house in St Mary's. I remember her.' And my mum said, 'Gary, I might not get out of here for a while and Ann said you can stay with her.'

When I heard Mum say that I knew something was wrong and said, 'When are you coming home?' and I then tried not to cry, saying, 'Mum, tell me you'll get better, and you'll come home soon.'

Mum had a tear running down the corner of each eye and she said, 'If something happens to me, Ann will look after you. She lives on a farm now and they have pigs and horses and there are children you can play with. You'll be alright with her.'

And as I cried, I said, 'I don't want to live on a farm, I want to live with you. You need to come home Mum. I need you.'

I was starting to shake, and Mum said, 'Son, you need to be brave,' and I cried out, 'Why do I need to be brave all the time?' and she said, 'Because you are my boy.'

I held Mum's hand and put my head on the edge of the bed until it was time to leave.

The rain was pouring down as I jumped in the back of Ann's husband's Land Rover. As I watched the water run down the windscreen, tears ran down my face and the car was quiet until we reached the farm. As we drove the winding country roads, I looked out to hundreds of yellow hay bales and there were big fences and stone walls with sheep and cows behind them.

The summer nights were long and there were sunburned children playing in the fields as we drove through the big gate to Ann's farmhouse. The rain had stopped as I was introduced to four children who had run and followed their dad into the yard and they were all happy to see me. There were two girls and two boys, and their faces were a rosy, red colour and their clothes were dirty, and strands of hay had stuck to their hair.

We went inside and we all had to get washed. We sat around a long wooden table and Ann's husband prayed while the children made funny faces at me. Ann brought over bowls of vegetables, and she had made a chicken pie and we all tucked in.

Straight after eating, we had to go and get washed again, and as the summer night's sun shone in through the bedroom windows, we were expected to go to sleep. I couldn't sleep as I lay there thinking about my mum and in the background, the room was filled with the noise of children snoring. I missed my mum, and I missed our council flat and as I stuck my head under the pillow, that's all I could think of.

The next morning, there was a sound of a bell ringing, and everyone jumped up and started running about. The children were running and trying to get dressed at the same time and I sat up and watched them. 'Gary, hurry up. Get up. You're coming with us.'

I stretched my arms up in the air and said, 'Where are we going?' and the children said all at once, 'We have to do our chores.'

They were like The Waltons off the TV, and I was expecting John Boy to wander in and pull me out of the bed.

I got dressed and when I came downstairs, there was a row of wellie boots at the bottom, and there was a pair waiting for me.

For the first few days, I followed the children around and they showed me how to keep the place clean and feed the animals and we carried big silver urns full of milk up to Ann's house and we had to unblock the stream so the water could flow freely. By the end of the week, I knew the routine and I didn't get in the way as much. After our chores, Ann's husband came back in his car and we had a big breakfast of eggs, bacon, milk and toast.

I was in a different world and no matter how hard I tried, it just wasn't the world I knew. My world was with my mum, and I longed to see her again.

We were outside all day, and we walked to the local shop and Ann gave us money for an ice cream and we played hide-and-seek for miles, making it impossible for anyone to find you.

This went on every day until one day, I was outside in the

field and Ann shouted on me. I walked over to the wooden fence and jumped over, and Ann shouted, 'Gary, hurry up, your mum is better. Get washed and we'll take you up to see her.'

I ran as fast as I could, up the stairs and down again, and we were on our way to see my mum.

When we got to the ward, the sun was shining in the big windows, and Mum's curtains were open, and she was sitting up in bed and she was looking like her old self again. As I got closer, I saw my sister and I ran to her. Ann and her husband waved at my mum and Ann made a sign with her hand as if she was saying, I'll call you, and she lip synced 'I'll leave you alone'. Mum smiled and her eyes filled up, and then they left to wait outside.

We stood on either side of our mum and Pat started to cry and she put her hand over her nose.

I said, 'Hi Mum, I missed you. You look much better.'

'I'm a bit sore but I'm fine. The food is terrible. They said I could go home soon. I want to go now, but they said I have to take it easy as it was a big operation.'

'Mum, you need to rest. We were worried about you,' said Pat

We cuddled each other, then it was time to go again. I jumped in the back of the Land Rover and this time the window was down, and the sky was blue and red, and the sun was warm on my face as we drove back to the farm.

I will always remember my time living on that farm.

I remember the children and how happy they were, and I remember the hay bales, the animals, the big table we ate at, and stepping in cow's shite every day, but most of all, I'll never forget the love I got from a family I never knew.

When we got home from the hospital, Mum was told she had to rest for a while so she couldn't go to work. She was cut from end to end, and her recovery was going to take some time. I tried to do whatever I could around the flat and after a while it became second nature. I never thought about it, I just did it.

We would sit down at night and watch the telly and when the news came on, there was always talk of the Soviet Union blasting us all to hell with the threat of a nuclear attack. I would lie in my bed at night and imagine some James Bond–type madman, sitting at his desk with his big fat finger over an even bigger red button, and I would see a huge mushroom explosion, then an orange blinding flash out the multi's window, and the building would tremble and then there was grey and black ash that would rain down over Dundee. From what we saw on the TV, it wasn't that hard to imagine.

When we moved into the multis I thought everyone in the scheme played tennis and it seemed everyone had a 'bat' but me, but I later found out this pastime was only when Wimbledon was on, and I was glad.

I was getting older, and I started to exercise. I wanted to train and be strong like Muhammad Ali, Joe Frazier, Davy Crockett and Ken Buchanan, and the idea I had in my mind was to get as strong as I could in case my dad came back so I could defend us.

I would do pull-ups on my bedroom door, and push-ups until my arms would shake. I bought a bowie knife from an army naval store in the town, and I would practise in front of the mirror, like I was one of The Three Musketeers. I kept it hidden under my bed, and every day I would get better, stronger, faster, just like Steve Austin did in *The Six Million Dollar Man*.

Money was scarce, and I would crawl under the front office of the local community centre and sneak into the weights room I met a lad there called Connie who was training to be a judo champion, and we became good pals and training partners.

Mum was getting better and she went back to the factory, and not long after, she started going out to work in the pub again. I told her that she was meant to be resting and she said, 'Ach, I've been resting for too long and we need the money.'

One night, I was cleaning around the flat. Normally I wiped down the kitchen first, then I would empty the ashtrays and scrub the black tar off, then I would finish by cleaning the toilet. As I passed my mum's bedroom, I noticed her bed wasn't made so I went into her room to make it.

As I puffed up her pillow, I found a silver wrapper with three squares of Cadbury's whole nut chocolate, and I put them on her bedside table beside the lamp. As I pulled the sheet straight, I noticed a bump at the side of the mattress. I stuck my hand between the sheet and the mattress and, to my surprise, I pulled out a sharp, pointed knife that had a brownish deer antler handle with white speckles around the blade. I held it for a couple of seconds then I put it back where it was, and I took the chocolate and placed it back under Mum's pillow.

We each had a knife at the side of our beds, and we never mentioned we had it. It was for him. If he ever came back, he was getting it.

It was pay day for my mum, and I had to meet her down at the shops to carry the bags up the road. As always we got crispy fish and chips before we 'trachled' up the road with our tins of beans and groceries to keep us going for another week. We were in a hurry as Mum was working in the pub and I had to get home to meet my pal Eck so we could catch the bus to training.

After sharing our fish and chips, Mum grabbed the trolley outside the supermarket and scooted up and down the aisles and I got one of the small baskets and found the aisle that had all the tins stacked up. I looked up and down to make sure no-one was there, and I bashed the tins of soup and peas and beans, making dents in them, I then went to the front desk and asked where the manager was. The man behind the counter said, 'I'm the manager, how can I help you son,' and I said, 'I was wondering if you get any money off if the tins are damaged.' He said, 'Yes. If there are any tins that are damaged, get your mum to bring them here and I will reduce the price.' I said thanks, and with the good news, I went back and damaged some more.

We got our bags, and the wind was brutal on our faces as we walked up the road. As the bags of tins got heavier, we stopped for a bit to let the circulation back into our cold hands.

When we got in the front door, Mum said, 'Gary, I have to get going now. Come and lock the door and remember and lock it when you go out.'

'Mum, you shouldn't be working like this.'

'We don't have a choice, we need the money. That's me off. See you tonight. Mind and put the chains on.' As the door closed, I locked it and put the chains on until it was time to leave and catch the bus.

Eck lived in St Mary's and we always caught the same bus, rain, hail, or shine, and we never missed a training session. We got off the bus and to get to the gym, we had to cut through a rusty chain-wire fence that led to a derelict railway track. There were strange noises and sometimes we would hear screaming in the distance behind the dilapidated brick buildings. We would take turns scaring each other in the dark, saying that there was a figure or a ghost moving past the windows. In the end, we would scare ourselves, and we ran as fast as we could until we reached the busy main road and up the side street was the boxing club at the top of the lane. We punched the bags and we punched each other, and we braced ourselves for the walk back along the railway track, as we listened for things that went bump in the night.

It was around nine o'clock when I got to the front door. It was raining outside, and the wind was howling up through the two lift shafts and it spilled into the stairs and landings, making an eerie, uncanny sound.

For years, I just couldn't escape his ghost. If I was out at night, I would get into the lift and I would put my front door key through my clenched fist. As the lift moved, I watched as the numbers lit up, and sometimes the lift would stop unexpectedly, and I would ready myself as the door slowly opened.

Sometimes the door would open, and I stared into darkness if the landing light was broken. It was scary and unsettling as I pressed the button ten times to close the lift door. Anyway, when I got out of the lift, I looked behind me, opened the front door and stepped inside. I hooked the chains on, and as I made my way to the living room, I switched on the lights. Whenever I was on my own, I would leave the living room door open so I could hear if anyone was at the front door, and that night was no different.

I knew he was gone, but like a phantom in the night, I always thought he would come back.

The wind was rattling through the letterbox and as I was watching the TV, I heard the click that the letterbox made when the postman put the bills through it. As I jumped up, I heard a voice that was creepy and dreamy, like the voice that Dracula made when he wanted the girl lying in the bed to come and open the window in the vampire films, 'Gaaaarrrrryy … Gaaarrryay!'

My name came whispering through the hallway and into the living room. I was instantly frozen with fear as I knew it was him. He was back. I paced the living room floor and the hairs on the back of my neck were bristling and I was shaking as I looked up the black void of the hall.

I was terrified as I thought that any minute now, he would come crashing through the door. I crept along, hugging the woodchip walls until I turned into my bedroom. I took my knife from its sheaf and the fear, adrenaline and anger inside me gave me the courage I didn't know I had.

The room was quiet and every time I took a step, each creak on the floorboards under the carpet amplified in my mind, and as I got closer to the front door, I was expecting the banging and chaos to start. As I reached the end of the hall, I gripped my knife and had a quick look around the corner of the wall and the letterbox was open.

I looked down and thought about how quiet and peaceful it was when he was gone, and I thought about my mum, and I thought fuck this, and I moved towards the door and shouted, 'Fuck off and leave us alone. I'll fucking kill you, you bastard,' and I rammed my bowie knife through the letterbox, hoping to stick him in the head.

I pulled the blade out and stepped back and all I could see was a shape through the wire meshed, frosty glass window in the door. As he walked away, I crouched down and looked through the letterbox and saw the emergency door slowly closing. I sat with my back to the toilet door and stared at the front door for hours, listening to the wind tinkling the letterbox.

I never heard from him again and I never told my mum what happened that night.

There were school halls opening their doors every Friday and Saturday night in every scheme, so we all had somewhere to go and dance. The music was powerful, and it had young boys and girls going crazy.

For me, getting money wasn't easy and I would go through the bins, 'raking' and picking out discarded lemonade bottles, and carry bags of them to the ice-cream van that would drive around every night, and he would give me two pence a bottle for my trouble.

The multis had thousands of families crammed into each block and every night there were children playing at the park and young boys and girls, wandering around, looking for somewhere to go. All we had was the chipper, the grocery store, and the community centre, and when the winter nights came in, we would walk around the scheme and then go and sit on the haemorrhoid-inducing emergency stairs of whatever multi we lived in, and talk shite and tell lies and wish it was Friday again.

Whenever I couldn't find enough bottles to go to the disco, I went with Mum to the pub, and I sneaked out of the back shop and walked around the dance floor of the disco. The women from the factories were all drunk and when they saw me, they pulled my arm and told me they would give me a few pence if I would dance with them. I moved around awkwardly until the novelty of dancing with a just turned thirteen-year-old wore off and I went back to watch the men hunched over the bar until their session on the stool was over.

I sat counting my hard-earned shrapnel and there was a man sitting at the bar that I had not seen before. He had an old teddy boy haircut that was in need of a good trim and he had a flat nose. He was wearing a workman's donkey jacket and I noticed the patches of leather on his elbows were resting in a small puddle of beer. As he sipped his nip of whisky, he was somewhere else.

I watched as the bar doors swung open and a young lad walked in and approached the man with the flat nose. As he got closer, he raised his hands up and I could see that his fingers were taped up with Elastoplasts and there were razor blades in between each finger.

The man sitting at the bar didn't see him coming and as he put his glass down, the younger man put his two razored hands around his face as if he was playing a game of peekaboo, and casually but violently ripped the man's face apart, then walked out of the pub.

Nobody, including the man, knew what had happened until the bar doors stopped swinging, and my auntie Cath shouted on my mum to get a towel. The man took the towel and mopped up the blood. The cuts were deep but the blood stopped flowing as much and the man left the pub holding his face in his hand.

I wondered to myself what he could have done for this kind of retribution. As my mum washed down the bar and my auntie mopped the floor, another regular started his shift on the stool and the music and dancing continued as if nothing had happened.

We kids all tried getting money any way we could. Some of us delivered newspapers, some of us got a job delivering milk in the mornings, and I got a job working in a butcher's back shop. For all of us, it was a means to an end.

One night, my four pals and I were sitting on the stairs talking about the weekend's disco that was only two days away. We all came from different backgrounds, but we were all working class. Nobody knew how poor I really was, and I wasn't telling them.

Jimmy said, 'I didn't get paid this week. There was some fuck up with the wages and I need to wait till next week, so I'm skint,' and Moe replied, 'You'll be alright as yer mum will give you money to keep you going. She always does.'

Charlie shouted over, 'Let's put our money together and see how much we can get for some beer,' and I said, 'We won't have enough for anything. I have been thinking and I have an idea. There is a brewery down the road in the industrial estate and I see trucks going in and out of there all the time. There must be loads of beer in there.'

Wee Jake looked at me and smiled and said, 'You're not thinking what I think you're thinking ...'

'Fucking right I am. Let's rob it. We could get a load of beer and we could sell some to get money. Do you fancy it?'

We all looked around the cold, graffitied stairwell and at each other and we chewed on our lips, as we contemplated the start of a career in crime. 'Wee Jake' said, 'Let's fucking do it,' and we all stood up and ran down the stairs.

We left the multi and walked down to the industrial estate. When we got there, we stared up at a ten-foot-high fence that had barbed wire around the top. We looked at each other and started to climb up and as we climbed higher, the more we looked at each other. We all got caught on the barbed wire, but we eventually got to the other side then, like true professionals, we fell on our arses.

As we walked away, Moe said, 'That was too easy,' and

Charlie shouted over as he stood looking at a gate with no padlock on it, 'Not as easy as this.'

The five of us looked at each other nervously, and kept walking into the loading dock of the brewery's warehouse. I found a door with a big glass window, kicked it in as quietly as I could, and we all crawled through.

The place was huge and there were boxes and pallets and hundreds of silvery grey barrels stacked around the floor, but they were all empty. It was difficult to see and the only light there was, was coming in through the roof from the car park flood lights.

We were about to lose hope, and just as Jimmy said, 'Where the fuck is the beer?' we saw a light go on in the far corner and Wee Jake shouted over, 'It's here! I found some beer.'

We rushed over and when we got in the small room, I said to Jake, 'Are you alright in the head? You do realise that we are not meant to be in here and you're shouting and telling the world we are? Anyway, where's the beer?'

'It's in here,' said Wee Jake, and he smiled a proud smile, opened the fridge door and pulled out a bottle of Skol lager and said, 'There's enough for one each.'

As we stood in the warehouse lunch room, we looked at each other, drank our bottle of lager and laughed. When we got through the broken door at the loading dock, we went to the gate that wasn't locked and walked through it. I thought about my simple plan and how dumb it really was, and came to the conclusion that there was never going to be such a thing as easy money for me. We walked up the road to the chipper, and the next day we all went back to our day jobs.

Mum had booked the washroom and I carried down her washing basket and, most of the time, I would stay with her as I didn't like leaving her on her own. It was noisy but it was warm and the fragrant lemon smell from the hot dryers and the washing powder made up for the banging of the clothes in the drums. Mum would tell me stories about when she was younger. She would never go into too much detail, but she told me she lived in a gypsy caravan when she was touring with the carnivals and one night, she had a visitor.

'Gary, in those days, I didn't drink. I was a young girl and my granny used to tell me that a ghost would be coming to see me throughout my life, and she told me that it was nothing to worry about as this ghost would come to see me three times in my life and the last time would be before I would leave this earth. I was lying in my bed and the caravan had a rounded roof and there were drapes of all colours that were pinned to the walls and across the roof. There was an old oil lantern in the corner of the room and when I looked over I saw a black figure at the corner of the door. It had no face or body, and it was just a shape. It picked up the lantern, brought it over to me and held the light over my head. I ducked under the covers, then stuck my head out to see if it was gone, and it was still there. I stared at the black figure, and it took the light away and disappeared into the corner of the caravan's door.'

'What happened next?'

'I went to sleep,' said Mum. 'I remembered what my granny said so I wasn't scared. I have to tell you something…'

'What is it Mum?'

'Last night that same ghost came back to see me, and it appeared from inside the corner of my bedroom door,' and I laughed and said, 'What, a ghost was upstairs in our house last night?' and Mum said, 'Don't laugh, the next time I see it will be before I die, and I don't want to die yet so the reason I'm telling you is so you never close my door.'

I laughed again and reassured my mum I would never close her door, and from that day onwards I let Mum make her own bed.

Every Thursday I read the *Evening Telegraph*, as it would tell you what films were on, and I would get the bus into the town and try and sneak into the pictures as much as I could

There was a film on at an old, run-down flea pit called The Vic, and from past experience, it was really easy to get under the counter and through the curtains. The film was *The Exorcist* and as soon as I ducked for cover and got inside,

I hid behind the curtains on the side and tried to get comfy as the film came on.

At first, I wondered if it was going to be scary at all and then I understood why there were people outside the pictures protesting about it and nuns with messages about God, preaching to the people in the line not to see it. As I peered through the smelly curtains, I looked at the screen and was mesmerised and terrified all at the same time. I liked it that much, I went back the next night.

I loved going to see the films and I tried to get into every picture house I could. One night, I sneaked into the wrong kind of picture. It was a small hole in the wall and there weren't many people in the line. I noticed a few strange-looking men as I got in.

I hid behind the curtain as usual and as soon as I heard the music, I thought that something was wrong. When the music stopped, I looked over at the men sitting in the chairs and they looked as if they were trying to find something in their pockets, then I looked at the screen and I couldn't believe what I was seeing.

There was a woman with no bra on and then another and they were actually naked. Not like the woman in the factory. Really naked. Then a man came on and he was walking about, and his willie was sticking upwards like the man that had chased me and Tommy down the burn. I had to get out of there.

As I got up and untangled myself from the musty-smelling curtains, I noticed the men in the chairs were now scratching themselves under their long raincoats and their eyes were glued to the screen. I crept out along the purple walls and through the smoke haze and the black velvety drapes to the foyer. I had sneaked into this place and now I had to sneak out. As I ran up the cobbled street, I hoped no-one saw me.

It was my mum's birthday and it had been a long time since she celebrated anything so she invited my aunties and uncles up, and a few pals to the flat, as she wanted to have a get-together.

Mum checked there was enough money in the meter as she put in the fifty-pence piece. She made all the food and there was 'stovies' (a Scottish potato stew), steak pie, homemade soup, and she made sandwiches with corned beef, egg mayonnaise, and prawns and cheese from a tube. There was a 'Party Susie' that had compartments of sweaty Scottish cheddar, pickled onions, cut up hot-dog sausages, and pineapple chunks to make it more exotic.

They all started arriving and dumped their coats in the cloakroom, which was the top of Mum's bed, and each person brought their own 'kerry oot', which was what they were drinking. As they all came in, they claimed their seat and settled in for the night.

In the kitchen, Mum was happy, and as she stirred the

bubbling pots on the stove, she would shout over the noise, making sure everyone was okay and had a drink. This was her domain.

The tiny kitchen was bursting with food and there were all kinds of drinks lined up along the floor. As soon as all the chairs and stools were filled, the records went on and the sounds of Del Shannon, Elvis, Neil Diamond and Shirley Bassey belted through the living room and also into the next-door neighbour's. Mum never sat down, and she hovered in and out of the kitchen serving people, and she ate and drank standing up.

The room was so hot from the stove and there was a thick haze of tobacco smoke. Every now and then, there was no choice but to open all the windows before we collapsed, and the cold night air would have people running to the bedroom to get their coats on. When the windows were closed again, condensation appeared instantly on the glass and the living room door, as the steam from the soup and the 'stovies' went through the room.

After a few hours of drinking, the singsong started, and as I stood, hiding in the kitchen, I watched my aunties and uncles close their eyes and, for two minutes, they transformed themselves and sang their hearts out like their favourite singers. As soon as they hit some kind of a note, the well-oiled audience in the room would shout out, 'C'mon Shug, give it 'laldy',' and with much clapping and knee-slapping encouragement, Shug became Del Shannon, and it was brilliant.

As the whole room stared at him, he sang, 'Don't ash meee, a mountain of questions, when there is only one anser to it allll … do hue love meee'. Shug took a swig of his can of lager before he readied himself for the big finale, and the crowd cheered and clapped until the end, and then he said, 'Ach, I was better the last time.' Everyone reassured him that he wasn't, and it was then on to the next person for their turn.

My mum loved singing and when she took the centre of the living room, there were oohs and ahhs and 'Here's Annie. C'mon Annie, what about 'Fools Rush In'?' When she started singing, she brought the house and the walls down with her emotional, ear-bursting rendition.

As she stood there, tapping her foot and waving her hand as she hit each note, she was in her element and at her happiest and, for just one minute, she had a sparkle in her eye as she winked at me.

Just Another Brick in the Wall

We all gathered in the playground of our new school. As we stood there, checking each other out, we had heard the stories about what big school was going to be like for us all, but before I got off the bus for my first day, I had made my mind up that I wouldn't be going there for too long. I was put into a class of boys who were all trying to find their way and some of them thought they had a reputation, and some wanted to have a reputation, then there were a few swats, a couple of quiet timid types, and me.

I hated it, mostly because I didn't understand what they were teaching me. I had lost too much time and I spent too much time looking out the window. All I wanted to do was work and get us some money to live. For me, it was a waste of time.

As soon as the bell rang in the afternoon, I ran from school to the butcher's shop to get my apron on and I would then report to the boss Rob and I would scrub the wooden blocks, clean the knives, wash the windows and help the men unload the trucks of beef. I never stopped and it seemed Rob's only business was keeping me busy for two hours. Just as the clock would strike six every night, and I had my apron off and my coat half on, he would ask me to do something else. I worked twenty hours for ten pounds, and he never paid me for the bit after six. It was a job and I never complained, nor did I have a choice.

Big school was proving to be daunting for a lot of boys, and I would see how cruel it could be for them just because they were a bit different. I tried to make the best of it as often as I could.

The bell rang and we all walked in lines to different doors that led to different corridors and into our classrooms. As I walked, I thought about running out the main gate and never coming back then I realised I was walking into two periods of maths class. We staggered through the door and sat down at the old wooden one-piece-fits-all-type steel frame that you had to squeeze your legs through before you sat down. There were decades of 'doofers' splattered across the ceiling above our desks, which were spit and phlegm mixed with paper that was munched in the mouth then

spat out into your hand then launched upwards at a rate
of knots. Every classroom had the same musty smell that
brought back memories of my dad's house and there was a
floor-to-ceiling blackboard that the teacher pushed up and
down. I stared up at the stained blotches of the roof and
looked at the chalk marks and numbers on the board and
then Mr O'Reary walked in. He was wearing a brown tweed
suit and he had a black cloak on that was trailing across the
floorboards. He was a short, stout man, with a head like a
horse, a cerebral mind and misanthropic tendencies.

Mr O'Reary never said much and as soon as he entered
the room, it was down to work. As he turned around to find
his stick of chalk, I thought about listening to him for an
hour and a half straight, and it was then I decided to launch
my substantial green and white rubber into the back of his
head. I took aim and watched the rubber missile hit and
bounce off then hit the wall. The direct hit had Mr O'Reary
spinning around like a top and he went absolutely off his
head, saying, 'Which one of you wee bastards did this?
C'mon then, who was it?'

The classroom was in shock and a few of the boys had
their mouths open. The teacher walked up every aisle
tripping over school bags, and as he stopped at every desk,
staring into the eyes of scared pupils, he said, 'Right you
bastards, if someone doesn't own up to this then I will not
teach you any more maths. You can all sit there and play
with your cocks for all I care.' The classroom erupted with

a mixture of sniggers and belly laughing and Mr O'Reary stormed out of the room with his black cloak following him. We all laughed and waited on him coming back but, true to his word, he never did. The bell rang and we all left happy, as gym class was up next.

I was in the playground, and I was talking to a boy when another lad joined us, and he had a cigarette butt hanging from the side of his mouth. I was carrying my gym shoes tucked into my arm, and as we talked I was looking the other way. Unbeknownst to me, the boy took the cigarette from his mouth and dropped it into my training shoe and stood back smiling. There was a burning smell and the boy started laughing. I was confused and took my shoe and emptied it until the smoking butt hit the concrete. I told the laughing boy he had better run and he stood there in defiance. I looked at the other boy standing beside me and turned away from him and hit the smoker once, breaking the boy's nose instantly. He fell back, staggering in shock, and as he held his nose, I thought back to my mum punching the woman in the 'backies' all those years ago. As I walked away, I said, 'He won't do that again.'

Before we knew it, maths was upon us again, and as we stepped into the class, Mr O'Reary was already there, sitting like a king on his throne, with his cloak sitting perfect as if someone had arranged it for him. He had his suit on, his hair was shining with grease, and he looked fitting for a portrait above a fireplace in a castle somewhere far, far away.

We all squeezed into our desks and Mr O'Reary said, 'I have an announcement to make. Young Mr McPherson has owned up to striking me with the eraser, and he will now be punished. What I am about to do should be a lesson to all of you. This will not be tolerated in this class. McPherson, up here boy to get your medicine.'

I was staring at Micky McPherson and I couldn't believe he had owned up to something he didn't do. Micky looked over sheepishly and shrugged his shoulders as he walked to the centre of O'Reary's stage.

As Micky stood there, looking across the class, O'Reary said, 'Right McPherson , you're getting six whacks for this, and you will feel every one of them. Get your sleeves rolled up.' He stepped away to his desk drawer to get his belt out, and we all sat there in disbelief, watching the teacher limber up, readying himself for some much-needed exercise. O'Reary looked over at us and smiled and said, 'This is going to hurt boy, now get your hands up and don't move. Micky raised his hands up and then the teacher ran six quick trots from the window and brought the 'tawse' of hard leather down on to Micky's hand, catching him up his wrist.

O'Reary's big head was red and there was a vein popping up from nowhere at the side of his swept-back grey hair. With every strike landed, the more frazzled he looked. Micky took his medicine, his hands ringing with pain, and as he walked back to his desk, he tried rubbing his hands together but couldn't, so he folded his arms and tucked them inside the armpits of his school jumper.

O'Reary was sweating and exhausted as he left the classroom and we all gathered around Micky, staring at the purple and black welts that travelled halfway up his arm and across his hands, and Micky said, 'Look what he's done to my hands! That horrible wee bastard is a maths teacher and he can't count. He said I was getting six and he gave me five.'

After the bell sounded, we took Micky to the sink and he ran cold water on his injured hands and I said, 'What the fuck were you thinking anyway? We had it made in there, and you owned up to something that wasn't even you.'

'Sorry, are we still pals?' said Micky. 'I was bored in there.'

And as we laughed and walked together, I thought to myself, Micky wasn't bored, he just wanted to learn.

Mum was standing in the kitchen, and I noticed she was very quiet and there was no music playing, which was unusual. I asked if everything was alright and Mum said, 'Gary, I know you wanted to be the same as everybody else, and go to Austria on the school trip, but I made the first instalment and there are too many bills coming in that I have to pay for and I thought I could find the money, but I can't now. I'm still paying for last Christmas so I just can't keep up with it all and the second instalment is coming up. We can't afford it. I'm sorry son.'

I saw Mum was getting upset and as she sat down, she started to sob and I said , 'It's okay Mum, I didn't really want to go anyway. Art galleries and statues, and all that *Sound of Music* shite. What's all that about? It's okay, I'll go another time, later on.'

Mum looked up, crying, saying, 'I know you wanted to go. I'm sorry, there's just too many bills for us and I can't keep up. I'm sorry son, but you will need to get a job, and in your life you will need to work for anything you get and nobody will give you anything. I pray every night, that things will get better for us.'

I reached over and hugged her, and a feeling came over me. There was no divine intervention, just a feeling that although I had been hearing my mum pray every night for years, I realised a long time ago that no-one was listening, and no-one would be helping us. In that moment, I knew what I had to do.

All the talk on the TV was about Scotland qualifying for the 1978 World Cup and there was even some talk of the team coming back with a medal. We were still going to the school hall discos and the music was sending us all crazy. Punk rock, northern soul, heavy rock and disco had us dancing every Friday and Saturday night and we were all doing whatever we could to find some money so we could dance. We drank our 'kerry oots' on the stairs and would walk the streets and end up at the chipper. With nowhere to go, we were all trying to belong.

I was dodging school, but I was still going in early to the butcher's back shop and the boss was still keeping me back every night, squeezing what he could out of me. When I asked Rob if he would give me extra hours after I explained our situation, he said he would look at it, but he never did.

One day, I was sitting drawing a plant or an old boot in art class and the headmaster came into the classroom, and with the art teacher, they asked me if I was interested in going into the town to meet the boss of the graphic arts department for our local newspaper. They said they wanted to encourage me to use what they described as 'exceptional talent' and I was very happy and excited as no-one had helped me before.

We got on the bus and the teacher took some of my drawings in a big folder. I was in awe as we walked up the stairs to the boss's office. I sat there in the fancy foyer and had visions of working there. I planned to tell Rob to get fucked as soon as possible, and I was looking forward to telling my mum that our money worries were over.

The big, shiny, wooden door opened, and a girl told me to go through. I walked into an even shinier office, and sat at a round desk. The boss introduced himself and proceeded to pull out the sketches I had done in art class.

The man was using words such as impressive and fantastic and I sat there and wondered what was going to happen next. The boss said to me, 'Gary, this is astounding detail, and you obviously have a special talent. You will definitely have a future in graphic design. I suggest you come back and see me after you finish college, and we can talk more.'

I smiled and said, 'Thanks for meeting me, but I need to go now, so I can catch my bus for work as I can't be late.'

I stood up and as I walked out of the man's office, I knew this day was never going to come for me. I was a pleb from the schemes, and as I ran my hands down the smooth timber furniture and railings, I realised this was just like the meaningless trip to Austria with its art galleries and culture club. I got to the bottom of the marble stairs and I threw my folder in the rubbish bin and I thought to myself, who the fuck would want to sit and draw all day for a job anyway. As I pushed open the big doors that led to the busy street, I could only hear my mum's voice in my head saying, Get a job and work hard, as no-one will give you anything in life, and anything you get, you'll need to work for it.' I had as much chance of finishing high school and going to university as Rob giving me extra hours, and Scotland getting a medal in Argentina.

My time at school was drawing in and I wanted to be there less and less. I hated most of the lessons and I particularly disliked history class, but the one saving grace for me was the history teacher, Mr Stanmore.

Stanmore was a well-spoken Englishman trying to teach

us history to the best of his ability, and to anyone who would listen, and he reminded me of one of the gentlemen you would see in *Tom Brown's School Days*. There was a sense of madness and chaos in his class, which always made it worth going. He would walk around swooshing his belt like he was sword fighting an imaginary foe at the blackboard and he would ask us random questions about history, or even football. If anyone gave him the wrong answer, he would get them up in the middle of the decrepit old room and belt their hands until he had satisfied himself that they were listening.

We would mess around and surround him and say, 'Listen Stanmore, don't you be messing with us. We are the Ardler boys and we take no shite, okay?'

He would laugh and push us out of the way and say in his best schoolboy accent, 'Well look at you. Young, fine Scottish men, full of spunk. Look at yourselves. As I stand here today, I see a bunch of Neanderthals from the housing schemes, and you can all be much more than that. I implore you to be better than that. Now move out my way you bunch of homos and sit down.'

Half the class sat down and fell asleep or pretended to, and the other half couldn't shut up. There were 'doofers' going right and left on the walls, and paper was ripped from books, which would be scrunched up and thrown across the room at each other. There was no control. We liked Mr Stanmore but one day he went too far and so did we.

Mr Stanmore stood front and centre and as he walked up the aisles, he slapped his leather belt up and over his shoulder, slapping the belt off his back, and he repeated this again and again as he said to us, 'Now listen here you fine bunch of Scottish cave dwellers, can anyone in this room tell me who Harald Hardrada was? He was a great man.' And the class was staring at him as we all knew where this was going, and it normally ended up with some poor bastard getting a few whacks of his belt.

'C'mon now, someone must know who he is. We read about him a few weeks ago in this very classroom. C'mon.'

The room was in silence until Stoney raised his hand, and as he looked across the room, he said, 'Did he play for United sir?' and the room erupted with laughter.

Stanmore walked to his desk and as he walked, he swooshed back his cloak like Batman and said, 'Right you young troglodyte, get up here. You're getting a few whacks for that.'

Stoney gave the class a nervous, awkward smile, pointed and clapped his hands together, and made a funny face. At this stage, Stanmore was pacing the floorboards and said, 'Stone, get your arse up here now. Just so you all know, Harald Hardrada was the last great Viking king and Stone has disrespected his name by trying to be funny saying he played for United, and we just can't have that.'

Stoney sat down then stood up again as his nerves were getting the better of him, saying, 'I'm not taking the belt for that, it was only a joke,' and Stanmore shouted, 'Get up here now boy!'

Stanmore walked to his desk, pulled out another belt and put the soft floppy one from his shoulder in the drawer. He held up this brand-new belt that none of us had seen before and it was brick hard and standing erect in Stanmore's hand. He started waving the rigid leather around like it was a Viking sword as he said to Stoney, 'Hurry up, let's get this done, and take it like the caveman you are.'

Stoney walked up and we started cheering his name, 'Stoney, Stoney,' and Stanmore told him to get his hands up and not to move a muscle or he would be getting more pain.

Stoney was now visibly shaking, and he said, 'I'm not taking the belt for this, it was only a joke' and Stanmore shouted, 'Get your fucking hands up boy!' and Stoney raised his arms and hands up, screwing up his face as he waited on the lash.

Stanmore stepped back until he was against the wall, and he ran like a warrior going into battle. Just as he was about to lash down hard, Stoney kicked him square in the bollocks. Stanmore stopped suddenly as if he had hit a wall and groaned. As he fell to his knees, he held his balls in his hands and fell over onto the classroom floor. A voice from the back of the room shouted, 'Pile on Stanmore ,' and the next minute, there was a tower of young boys on top of him. There were people falling off and more were having a go and then the bell rang for the end of the period, and we all fell off awkwardly then looked at each other in an 'Oh fuck' moment.

As we left the room, Stanmore wasn't moving but he was still groaning, and as we walked down the corridor of windows, we expected to be rounded up one by one, but nothing happened and I never saw our teacher Mr Stanmore again until years later, in a dive of a pub, and he was sitting on a stool at the bar, getting drunk on his own.

Not too long after that, I left the school. I was painting my mum's living room glass door, and as I was edging around the frosted leaves in the glass, the phone rang. It was my guidance teacher Mr Ford and he was calling to find out why I hadn't been going to school and if I was alright. I told him our situation and that I had to get a job so I could help out with money and we could catch up with the bills, so I wouldn't be coming back to school.

He told me that my mum could get into trouble from the social work department, and I told the teacher that I knew all about what they could do and that this was my decision, not my mum's. He asked me if there was anything he could do to help us, and I told him there wasn't and I thanked him for being a good teacher and hung up. I never heard from anyone again and that was the end of school for me, but it wasn't the end of lessons and learnings; in fact, it was just the beginning.

My mum started selling Avon cosmetics in the pub and the factory. She would hand out small brochures and the women would place an order and then there would be loads of boxes delivered to our flat. Mum would put the orders into bags, and we would carry the bags down to the factory and the pub and Mum would collect the money. A woman then came and paid Mum her commission. It was a lot of work for her but the flat smelled great.

At night, we would get all the bags with the orders and Mum would have the woman's name stapled to her bag. From there, it was down the multi's lift and into the back of a taxi and then straight into the back shop of the pub. My mum would go to work at the bar, and I sorted the bags out so they were ready to be collected. I hated Mum doing this, but it was a means to an end.

One night when I was sorting the bags out, I heard my uncle Joe's voice and as usual he came into the back shop to see me. As he walked in, he shaped up as if he was coming to fight me, saying, 'Hello son, how's yer training going. You're getting a big lad. How's the boxing going?'

I shaped up and said, 'Good. I'm training hard and I'm running down to the butcher's every day so I'm feeling good.'

Uncle Joe said, 'That's good. You're smelling nice anyway. How's your mum?' and I told him she was over doing it again and that I was worried she would get sick again. I told him that I was looking for a job and I had stopped going to school. He looked at me and rubbed his chin then he said, 'Do you fancy doing a bit for me? You can't tell anyone, and

I'll explain it to you as we go, and I'll show you the ropes, but you cannot tell a soul, okay son. Do you understand?'

I was listening intensely, and I said, 'Do I get paid?' And Uncle Joe shaped up again, and replied as he laughed, 'Of course you get paid you cheeky bugger. Now I'll see you later and go through what you need to do, but now I need to …' and at that point, I said, 'See a man about a dog.' He threw a left hook into thin air, smiled and said, 'Something like that son.'

As he was leaving, he dodged two thin men pushing a clothes hanger along the linoleum floor in front of the bar, and it was packed with leather jackets, suits and dresses and the tops were covered in clear plastic. Uncle Joe said 'Hurry up and get what you've got sold as you need to be out of here quick,' and then he was out the door.

A crowd had formed around the two men, and they were frantically taking in money and handing over the coathangers of garments. Within five minutes, everything was sold, and they were out the swinging doors of the pub.

I met Uncle Joe in a cafe in the town and the rain was pelting down so hard that the seagulls had their umbrellas up. We sat down and we had a sausage and egg roll and he explained what I had to do. 'Gary, you need to sit in a van, and I'll give you a book to write in and you need to write down when anyone goes into the building and when they come out. I need times so if he goes in at twenty past eleven, then you write that and same when he leaves. It has to be exact. I'll be with you, but I have to go, so you'll have to be on the ball okay.' I told him I could do that and we finished our breakfast and drove to the building. Uncle Joe parked back a bit, behind two cars.

The rain was heavy, and it was damp and cold inside the van as I leaned against the metal frame. Every now and then, I had to wind down the window so I could clear the condensation, and the rain soaked me as I waited for the window to defog. I watched and I waited, and I did what I was asked, and I was so happy when Uncle Joe handed me a crumpled up ten-pound note as he said, 'Well done son. Remember, keep this between me and you.' And I did.

Sometimes I would take orange envelopes and drop them off at people's offices, and sometimes I would sit in a car or a van and watch women who looked like Avril. As soon as her husband drove out the driveway, another car would arrive and the woman would meet him at the door and she would always kiss him like it was her last kiss on earth, and the man would normally grab her on the arse with both hands before they went inside.

I would get paid and I would go into Mum's kitchen and when she wasn't looking, I would put money in her jar and leave without saying anything. This went on for two years.

The winter was freezing cold, and they said it was the coldest winter in sixteen years. There were severe storms outside, and as we watched the TV, it seemed like everyone was on strike, including the gravediggers, so even the dead couldn't get buried.

The news called it, 'The winter of discontent', and as Mum and I sat eating our dinner, little did we know what was around the corner for us and the working-class people of not just Dundee, but the whole of the United Kingdom. They would need to brace themselves for a tsunami that no-one saw coming.

DISINTEGRATION

It was 1979 and there was violence in the schemes. Unemployment was high and as Madness was singing about going one step beyond, it seemed we were all going backwards. Scheme gangs were rising from the tenements and young men were following grown men into a pointless war on the street corners; Peter Pan types taking lost boys into a land that was never going anywhere. They had no money, no job and I think it was just a sign of the times, and a chance for all of them to belong to something; a voice of unreason to say 'fuck you' to the government, the police, and anyone else who stood against them. The scheme gangs were all colour-coordinated thugs and they would wear their own battle attire that women would make for each of them. I used to picture all these wee women sitting in their front rooms at sewing machines, spinning these cardigans for carnage, and I couldn't understand it. I stayed far away from them as much as I could, but most of the time it was impossible to escape.

We were still walking about the streets and drinking our cans of lager on the stairs. We would look at the Tennent's Lager girls on the back of the can as we sank every one we had, and we would venture out into the night and down to the chipper for a white pudding supper and crispy chips, with copious amounts of salt and vinegar, and after that, whatever happened, happened.

One day, we were all playing football on the orange gravel of the all-weather pitch that was down the road from the multis and as we played, we heard a huge roar in the distance and there were sounds of glass breaking and screaming. The game stopped and we all watched a large group of young men carrying sticks and stones in their hands. As they walked together, it was a sea of brown and yellow as the gang swung their arms and marched up the road towards us.

We huddled together, and I said, 'Look at these wankers,' and my pal said, 'Look up there, there's more. This is going to be on for young and old. Do you think we should run?' And I said, 'I'm not running from these bastards. They're not here for us, they're here for them.'

As we stood there, the leaders of the angry mob passed us and asked us to join them and they were moving that fast, they never gave us a chance to say yes or no so we stayed where we were. There must have been at least seventy of them and they were so fired up. I wondered why. The other mob were a sea of purple and sky blue, and they started running down the hill until the two gangs clashed somewhere in the middle of the children's play park.

There were arms and legs going hammer and tong, and bricks and stones were raining down, hitting the young and old. There was blood and a couple of them lost an eye. The police cars came across the grass from either side and there was a lot of running away in the heat of their battle. The wounded were scraped up off the concrete and the grass and taken away and we all shook our heads in disbelief, as we kicked the ball to the centre of the pitch.

I got home that night and asked my mum if she saw or heard anything out our kitchen window and I told her what happened, saying, 'Mum, we were playing on the pitch down the road and these gangs passed us and started fighting and there were a lot of boys badly injured and a couple of them lost their eyes and what for Mum!'

Mum said, 'You need to stay away from them. Stay away from those gangs, do you hear me?'

'I am, I do. I'm trying to but they are everywhere.'

'They are bullies, and if any of them ever come at you and hit you, you need to hit them harder so they remember not to bother you again. Stay away from them if you can as we don't want any more police at this door. We have had enough trouble.'

We both sat down to eat our dinner and, as usual, we watched the news. There was no talk of any gangs in the schemes, kicking the shite out of one another. The headlines for the day were about the IRA planting a bomb on a boat that killed the second cousin of the Queen, Lord Mountbatten, and six other people just off the coast of Ireland, near Sligo, and then later on, they blew up eighteen British soldiers at a countryside border crossing.

I thought about the destruction, the unrest, the violence and the sadness of raging war, and the photos of death and real carnage on the telly, and what was it all about? I thought about the dozens of boys getting stitched up in hospital and the two boys who had lost their eyesight, and I sat in bewilderment and wondered what the fuck was going on. It was a crazy time for all of us and after a while you realised that you just had to get on with it.

I was on the bus going into town and I was with my pals, Bob and Jimmy, and the bus was half full. We always sat upstairs at the back of the bus so we could get a bit of a view, and as we were turning the corner to a long downhill street, Bob made eye contact with a well-known thug who was standing on the street dressed in the usual skinhead wear which was jeans up to his shins and tucked into sixteen-hole Doc Martens bovver boots, and a white T-shirt and black braces. Bob thought it would be a good idea to wind him up and he unbuttoned his jeans, dropped them to his knees, jumped up on the back seat and stuck his warm arse against the window. Bob was laughing at us as we scrambled to the window and as the bus took off, the enraged thug ran after the bus, and we all laughed until the bus slowed down and came to a stop to pick up a line of people that were waiting. Bob instantly went into panic mode, saying, 'That big fucker is gonna catch the bus! He's running like Allan Wells ... he must be on something!'

And as the thug got closer to the bus, it took off again, and the laughing continued. We were all dancing about the bus then the bus slowed again. I looked out the side window to the street and the line to get on the bus was long, and the Olympian thug was closing in again. His arms were pumping, and his face was red, and it looked like his head was about to burst. As he banged on the back of the bus, the three of us looked down on him and the bus took off again, and me and Jimmy joined Bob and dropped our jeans and gave the thug a fitting farewell.

Margaret Thatcher was voted in as Britain's first woman prime minister, and over the years, each time the Conservative party had run England, and the rest of her isles, Thatcher had been there in the background. She was responsible for a few things in her career as she came up through the ranks, and one of the things she implemented was pulling the plug on the free bottles of milk I used to love when I got to nursery school.

The unions had beaten all before her, but she had big ideas to break them, and in doing so, she would create her own kind of anarchy that tore communities apart in the schemes and beyond. My mum hated her and if she came on the TV, she would say, 'Gary, get that bastard off. I can't stand the sight of her,' and I would laugh. For whatever reason, Mum couldn't stand the Queen either. I would sit there and listen to my mum go on and it was funny.

Thatcher was one thing, but to me, the Queen was just a lady who used to wear funny hats and come on the telly at Christmas before *The Wizard of Oz*, and as far as I was concerned, she never did anything wrong. But Thatcher was doing plenty as she steadily closed industries down, and she made hard-working men a dying breed, to make way for her privatised nation of technology parks and nuclear plants.

Depression and recession hit us as hard and as fast as a belt in the puss, and she was just getting started.

It was winter and there was snow lying on the ground and occasionally there were flurries blowing through. As we looked up at the thousands of lit-up windows in the council blocks, we could see hundreds of children looking out of their bedrooms at the powdery blanket of snow below, hoping that it wouldn't rain while they slept so they could get outside and build snow men and ice castles in the morning.

We had left the stairs and it seemed warmer outside than it was sitting on the freezing steps of the multis. The five of us walked through the snow and stopped for a pee and as we stood, we wrote our names in yellow, into the snow. We walked down to the chipper and were all debating what greasy, heart-attack inducing delicacies we were having when we got there.

As we rounded the corner, the snow outside had melted and there was black slush, creating a pathway into the entrance of the shop. There were seven skinheads standing outside, and a few of them were eating chips. They stared at us and we walked past them. I knew the leader from the boxing, and I acknowledged him, by giving him a nod and a quick smile.

We ordered and, as usual, I asked for a white pudding supper, crispy chips and two pickled onions. We all paid and took our soggy-newspaper-wrapped food out into the cold. As I was last to walk out, due to waiting on the man cooking extra crispy chips, the skinheads made a wall around the door and one of them stepped forward from the side and head butted me in the eye.

I looked at him and I was confused as to why he did this as I gave him no reason to, so I punched him, and he fell backwards into the snow-covered concrete pavers. The skinheads helped him up and made a bit of circle around me and he was angry at all the fuss he was receiving, and he snarled at me, 'I'm gonna fucking kill you.'

I waited until he moved, and I slipped to the side and knocked him down with an overhand right and he crashed against the bakery's window. I walked away and as I turned around, my white pudding supper was gone and so were my four pals.

The leader of the skinheads shouted over at me, telling me that this wasn't finished yet, and they helped up their shell-shocked pal. I walked down the road, past the shops, and through to the community centre gates. The seven skinheads followed me, and started chanting, 'Pain is the game, pain is the game.' As I turned around, one of them ran at me and tried to tackle me, and I rolled him over and punched him in the head four times then stood up and walked off the black slushy path and into the darkness and white snow of the playing fields.

The moon and a few streetlights shone down on the snow, and the gang all continued to follow me, while chanting, and I thought I was about to get hammered or worse.

I stopped again and turned around and the skinhead said, 'Pain is the game, and we are not finished yet,' and I said, 'He's had enough, fuck off and leave me alone.' The skinhead walked into the light and said, 'I'm gonna fucking do you,' and I hit him flush on the nose and he fell over on to the snow and his face was a mess.

The skinheads started getting really rabid and they were hungry for someone else's blood. The bonehead leader said to me, 'Kill him. Pain is the game. You need to finish him, or we will finish you.' They were getting so far out of control with the chanting and their body language that I realised they were all off their heads on drugs and alcohol, and I had to do something to show them I was crazier than them, and do it quickly.

I stood back and they helped up the battered skinhead, and no matter how much drink or drugs were inside him – most of it was punched out of him –he still came forward.

I punched him and jumped on top of him and as the chanting was getting louder and more intense, I was getting tired, and decided to try and end it. I bit down as hard as I could on the skinhead's tight skin of his big forehead, and I ground my teeth together until I broke through the layers of his brew, and I tasted the metallic tang of blood on my tongue. When I could feel his flesh in my mouth, I ripped the piece out, spat it at the leader and said, 'Are you fucking happy now?' I pushed myself off the skinhead and there was blood all over the snow-covered ground. I turned and walked up the road and when I got far enough away, I picked up a handful of snow and bit into the snow cone and washed my mouth out and washed the skinhead's blood off my face.

I looked back and each of them was still chanting, and they were taking turns kicking the ruined skinhead as he lay there tossing around in the blood and snow. As I reached the bottom of the multi, the snow started to fall heavily, and I had never been so happy to be home.

The next day, I went into the town Christmas shopping for Star Wars toys, and I was wearing a warm coat, a black eye, and a chipped front tooth.

It was a time of unrest, and the economy had started to collapse. With the factories closing down, thousands of people would line up outside 'the brew' or 'the social' and sign on to claim what they could from the government. Some got so used to living off 'the brew', they didn't even try getting a job, and after a while, signing on became part of their lives. Hard working men were broken and forgotten and all they had was their pride and getting a few pints on a Saturday afternoon before going to watch the football.

For me, I didn't have much but Mum was happy, and I had enough to get a 'kerry oot' for the stairs, and money for the chipper, and just enough so I could dance and get lost in the music.

In hard times, we all need something to believe in and for me, it was training hard. My inspiration was the World Lightweight champion, Jim Watt, and the film *Rocky II*.

As soon as the film came out at the pictures I went to see it the first night it played, and I was captured by the struggle and the story. I don't know why, but I always rooted for the underdog, and when everybody wanted to be the cowboy, I wanted to be the Indian; when we were playing football, I would volunteer to play at the back when everyone else wanted to score goals; as I lay on my bed listening to music, I would focus on the drummer, not the singer. I'm sure this was some kind of psychological thing in me, but I think I was just born to be the underdog.

We were all looking for something that wasn't there so we

tried our best to have as much fun and to laugh as often as we could. We would walk around the schemes, dodging the loonies, the gangs and the dog shite, and we would venture into the unknown that was, 'plundering'.

We would walk down to the vast green and yellow fields beyond Dundee, and as we walked along the winding country roads, we must have stuck out like lemons, looking for the farmers' apple trees. One of us would climb the tree and shake and pull and strip it until it was bare. Sounds easy enough, but like breaking into the brewery, sometimes crime just didn't pay. It was the farmer versus us and, more often than not, he won, as we would be chased through unfamiliar territory of cows'-shite landmines, and we would be caught and taken prisoner before the local police came and they kicked us where it didn't show and sent us home with sore arses.

Occasionally, we would win, and as we gathered up and loaded the apples into our jumpers, we would run and hide and all gather around to taste our bounty, hoping that at least one was the golden apple, but it never was.

Swimming was another pastime we did and, other than the obvious, we went there mostly to get out of the cold. It was also the chance to see girls in their swimming costumes or, if we were lucky, women in bikinis. The showers were roasting hot and as we walked out of the steamy building, the cold wind blew your hair back, and we walked to the chipper to get a bag of chips for the bus ride home, and it was magic.

I was still working in the butcher's and Rob was still telling me he would try and increase my hours but every night he was still asking me if I could do one more job for him as I was leaving. I was still getting a few days with my uncle Joe and at night, when my mum was working in the pub, I would watch 'The Rockford Files and Baretta and I thought to myself, I could do that.

Uncle Joe met me in our usual place, and we ordered bacon and egg rolls. As we were waiting, he said, 'How's yer training going,' and I replied, 'Good. I'm doing a lot of road work and I'm enjoying it,' and he said, 'You should get down to the swimming and start doing some underwater training as it's good for the lungs. Ken Buchanan swears by it.' The woman brought our rolls over and we tucked in.

As soon as we finished eating, he said, 'Son, have you any ideas about what you are going to do in the future?'

'I was hoping I could keep working with you as I know how things work now.'

He looked at me and smiled, and said, 'You only think you know how things work, but it's not what you think son. There's a lot more to this life than going to the post office and delivering letters and watching 'hoors' shagging other men when their husband is away on the oil rigs. There is another side. A dodgy side, and people you don't want to deal with, and I don't want that for you. I don't want you living this life. It's not for you. You've always been a good worker and you can do better than this.'

I was deflated as I looked down at my egg-stained plate, and said, 'Better doing what Uncle Joe? There's no jobs out there. Look at the people hanging around the streets in the schemes. There's nothing for me.'

'What about getting a job in the butcher's? You've worked there for a couple of years and let's face it, people will always eat meat so that would be good for you. Have a word with your boss and see what he says.'

I looked up and said, 'I've been asking that prick for extra hours for ages and he has no intention of giving me anything. If he could, he would keep me there doing what I'm doing forever.'

Uncle Joe stood up and said, 'I'm sorry Gary, I don't want you doing this. It's not for you.' He went and paid the woman and I walked outside and waited on him to start work.

I didn't bother asking Rob for anything, but I decided to take Uncle Joe's advice and I walked to every butcher shop I could find and left my phone number, hoping to get a call, but they all said the same thing: that there were no jobs going but to keep trying and come back next week. So I did.

After a couple of months, I was given an opportunity working on the government's 'YOP' scheme to get young people off the 'brew' and I took it.

I worked for Rob up until the end of the week as I wanted

to finish on a good note. As usual, on my last day, just as I was getting my coat on to leave, he asked me if I could do one more job for him. I smiled at him and zipped up my coat and said, 'Not tonight Rob,' and he had a look of surprise and anger, and he said, 'If you don't, then there are plenty other boys that will, so get that coat off and do what I tell you.'

I looked at him, smiled, and walked out without saying a word, down the three steps into the cold wind that was howling up the Lochee road.

I started in the butcher's factory the following Monday and I worked sixty hours a week for thirty-one pounds. Like my mum, I never had a choice. I put my head down and worked harder than everyone else, and I watched and learned everything I could. As I sawed up the bones on the ban saw, swept the floors, scrubbed the benches with sawdust and steel brushes, and unloaded the beef trucks, I thought about sitting in that shiny office, drawing and designing colours from my imagination, in a world that was never going to be.

If there wasn't already enough sadness, unrest and violence going on, we watched the TV in disbelief, as the newsreader told us that the police had found another girl's body in Templeton Woods, and they said that the body was found close to where another girl was found the year before. They said there was a serial killer on the loose and they named him the 'Disco Killer'.

There was a quiet hysteria in every scheme across Dundee. If women had to go out for work, or out with their pals, or to the bingo, as they left, they would tell each other that they would ring the phone three times when they got home so they knew that each of them got home safely. When Mum went to work in the pub, she would call me to tell me she was leaving in the taxi, and I would meet her at the bottom of the multi and we went up the lift together.

The gang's and the skinheads were still kicking the shite out of each other, and we were all dancing to different tunes.

One night, Mum and I sat down to watch the news and eat our dinner and there was a news flash, saying that the nation was going to war. They showed footage of paratroopers marching with Bergen backpacks, and carrying machine guns across flat barren lands. The man on the TV said that the longer the conflict, the more troops they would need, and this would mean calling on the fine young men of Great Britain to see some action. Mum had just sat down and I said, 'Look Mum, the man on the news was just saying that they might need to call on the young men of Britain to fight in this war.' Mum said, 'You're not going anywhere, or to any war, you're staying here with me.'

I ate my dinner and watched more pictures of soldiers walking in miserable conditions. The wind was pushing them back as they trudged through the wet mud and gun ships and helicopters were moving through grey skies and black seas.

The next morning, I looked out the window and it looked cold outside. I made my way up through the block of council flats to catch my bus and when I got to the bus shelter the snow was falling horizontally. In the distance the bus lights were shining a frosty glow as the wheels navigated through the slush and the salt and the black ice. I stood waiting and thought about how the skinheads and the gangs would go fighting not in their own backyards but in a freezing cold land so far from home.

I jumped off the bus and the snow was heavy on the ground, and I ran up the road and through the laneway into the back shop of the factory. It was a Wednesday, and this was the day that brothers, Jim and Norrie Muir, delivered the fore legs and hind legs of beef. I loved talking to them as they would tell me stories about working in the slaughterhouse.

They were huge men and one day, I was sitting on a milk crate eating a sandwich and I gave Jim a bit of cheek and he came over to me and gently grabbed my butcher's overall, lifted me off the crate and into the air, smiled then put me down again.

I timed my tea break so I was sitting waiting for them in the loading dock and when they arrived, I would try and impress them as I helped them unload the heavy beef sections onto the hooks hanging on the overhead rails.

'Hi Jim, hi Norrie, do you need a help?'

Jim would always say the same thing, 'Hi son, are you on your break? We're okay, go and finish yer sandwich.'

And I would always reply, 'I'm okay, I want to help. It's good for my training,' and I would 'shape up' like my uncle Joe, and they would both laugh and say, 'Alright Rocky, you're a strong boy, so c'mon then.'

I had learned as much as I could in the butcher's factory and I had been thinking about asking the brothers if there were any openings with them and I was waiting for the right moment.

As I lifted off the last hind leg, I followed Jim to the side of the truck and said, 'Jim, are there any jobs going in the slaughterhouse? I'm a hard worker and I'm strong. I heard the money was better than here.'

Jim pulled out his pen and wrote down some numbers in his notepad, and said, 'Call this number. They are looking for someone and me and Norrie will put a word in for you. Good luck son.'

I said thanks and I held on to that piece of paper like it was a rare diamond or a secret document that no-one could see and I couldn't stop smiling at the thought of getting out of that place.

As soon as the truck left, I ran to the post office across the road and I called the number. Two weeks later, I started in the slaughterhouse at the docks and as far as I was concerned, there was a time and a place for everyone to make their mark, and now, it was mine.

From Youth to Uncouth

From the first day, I loved working in the slaughterhouse. My job was unloading the refrigerated articulated lorries that were packed with sides of beef that came from Ireland, London, and the west coast of Scotland. Once the beef was unloaded, they were hooked up on overhead rails and pushed in their hundreds to hang inside massive fridges.

I was on a mission to work hard and I treated it like training. I would saw and cut down fifty sides of beef every day and I loved the work. It seemed everyone was a character and they all had a story to tell; and although the job was physically gruelling, I jumped out of my bed every morning and couldn't wait to get there.

The money was double what I had been on and I had weekends off, which was a new experience for me as I had been working every Saturday since 1977 so it was like being on holiday every week.

At the end of the shift every Friday, one of the bosses would stand at the big wooden butcher's blocks and we would all stand in a line and he would hand us a parcel of six sausages, one pound of steak mince, a few pork chops, and a pound of stew, and he would thank us for the week's work. I was so happy to get home to show my mum the fruits of my labour.

I went into town and looked around for the biggest chest freezer I could find and I paid cash for it. The man in the shop said his people could deliver the same day and I made sure I was home when the doorbell rang. 'Mum, there's someone at the door,' I shouted. Mum answered saying to the men, 'What, a chest freezer for me?' and I met her at the door and said, 'It's for you Mum.' 'Is it not too big for us?' and I said, 'No Mum, I'm going to fill it for you. We will never be hungry again.'

I watched and learned from the old-timers, and after a few months I was one of them and I was part of the meat porter's crew. On my breaks, I would go into the fridges and punch the sides of beef, trying to crack the beast's ribs, and I realised *Rocky* made it look easier than it was, but every day I tried anyway. After a while, I noticed that everyone had an angle, a scam, a fiddle and it seemed as if it was normal practice, all the way from the killing halls to the butcher's front window.

It was an early start and once the trucks were unloaded and the beef was hanging straight on the rails, and the orders were out on the delivery trucks, then it was a case of hosing the blood down the drains and steam cleaning the concrete floors and white walls until you could eat your dinner off it, and then we all went home.

As I walked along the road to catch the bus, I could see a new wave of sons and daughters who had flooded out the school gates, trying to get as far and beyond as their mothers and fathers had tried to or had done; but as I saw them all standing around and waiting in line at the dole and the social office, something had happened on the way from the school gates that darkened and muddied their plans.

Thatcher had her own plans of using them up on the YOP schemes and nothing else mattered. Sign on the 'brew' and look for a job that wasn't there unless they had 'experience' – and what sixteen-year-old leaving school had any work experience? The only job you didn't need experience for was the army, as once you joined up, they would give you six weeks basic training and send you off to Belfast. To me, it was crazy, as they would let you shoot a gun, but they wouldn't give you a job in a shoe shop.

When I got home, I would lie at our two-bar fire and listen to my cassette of *Face Value* and as Phil would sing about roof's leaking, and missing out on love, I would think about me and my mum's future. When the room got dark that was my cue to get ready to go out running and as I ran through the dark streets, I thought about what tomorrow would bring.

I met Frankie when I started in the slaughterhouse and we became good pals. One day he called me and said, 'Gary, I need a hand. I have a deer and I need help getting him into my van. We need to get it back to my place so we can cut it up. We should make a few pound each. Can you help me?' I said, 'Okay, I'll be at the bottom of my multi in ten minutes,' and I hung up the phone.

As I got to the bottom, it was getting dark and the sweetie papers were swirling around then resting in the putrid puddles of piss in the dark corners of the concrete columns. Frankie drove down the road and the front of his van was bashed and there were traces of grass clumps embedded into the broken mirror. He waved me over and I jumped in the van. I looked behind me to the white interior of the transit van, and said, 'Where is he?'

'Who?'

'The fucking deer! Who did you think I was talking about?'

'Uh, he's up the road lying in the long grass and we need to go and pick him up, so we need to hurry.'

Frankie drove off and for a while, I wondered where he was taking me, but soon after, we pulled over and jumped out. The deer was lying soft and heavy in the grass and as we touched him, he was still warm.

I asked him what happened to his van but I already knew, and Frankie told me he was out visiting a lady friend he knew and occasionally he would go up and see her when her husband was away working on the rigs, which sounded familiar, and she lived in the country with her pet cat and a poodle. Frankie said that she was lonely and shrugged his shoulders as if to apologise. He told me that after he left her, he drove around a tight corner of the country road and he hit the deer head on, knocking it into the grass.

By the time he told me the story it was pitch black and we started to drag the dead animal from the side of the road. The deer was heavy, and it was wet and slippery, and we were falling all over the place as we wrestled it to the back of the open doors of the van. Frankie said, 'Fucking thing doesn't want to go in.'

'I don't think it likes you. Maybe if you tell it you're sorry for ploughing into it, it might want to jump in the van so we can get the fuck out of here.'

We both laughed and Frankie said, 'Fuck off you. C'mon, we need to get it in the van.'

We eventually got the deer into the van and drove away through complete blackness until we saw civilisation and streetlights in the distance.

We drove through streets with rows of houses and every time he slowed down, I thought we would be stopping. As

Frankie drove closer and closer to a big block of multis I said, 'I thought you lived in a house.'

'No, I've lived in the multis all my life,' he said proudly.

'I didn't mean that, what I meant was, it would have been helpful if you told me that you lived in a building with a lift, especially knowing that we have to take a dead animal up in it. Fuck me Frankie! It's a six-foot-tall stag deer, not your girlfriend's chihuahua!'

Frankie smiled and said, 'It's not a chihuahua, it's a poodle. C'mon, we'll be fine.'

We dragged the deer along the concrete at the bottom of the multi and there was a trail of wetness that we left behind. As we pulled and pushed the heavy load in through the lift doors, we stood on each side of the beast and propped it up like he was a drunk uncle at a wedding. Frankie pressed the light for the sixth floor and the door closed.

We looked at each other past the deer's nose and we looked upwards, hoping the lift would take off, but it didn't move, and a split second later, the lift door opened and outside in the foyer was an old lady with a face like a crumpled shirt from a Saturday night on a Sunday morning. She stared at us and the deer standing in the middle, and she got in with her shopping bags and pressed the number one on the lift panel and the door squeaked shut and two seconds later, she got out. When the door closed, we laughed until we reached the landing of the sixth floor.

Frankie covered the bathroom in plastic like in the

gangster films, and he spread his mum's towels over the small sink, and we propped the deer up in the corner of his bath and there were spiky bits of hide, skin, maggots, and blood everywhere. We both stood there shirtless as Frankie took off the animal's head and antlers.

I asked him where his saw and knives were and he told me they were in his bag downstairs in the van, saying, 'I'll finish this, if you can go down and get the bag.' When I returned, Frankie had been busy, and as I stood in shock, I said, 'Frankie what the fuck have you done,' as there was a bath full of hot red blood sludge that was ever so slowly gurgling down the hole in the bath. 'Frankie, is that hot water, please tell me you didn't use hot water or we will be fucked.'

Frankie smiled his usual laid-back stupid smile and said, 'I wanted to give him a bath to wash all the shite off before we cut him up. You worry too much Gary.'

'You know this deer belonged to somebody and if they find out that one of their animals is here, then the law is, they can take the van that took him away and they can take your house, so yes I am worried.'

And after all that, Frankie replied, 'Who cares, it's not my van, it belongs to the slaughterhouse, and this isn't my mum's house, it's the council's so stop worrying.'

I tried to unblock the plug hole but most of the congealed blood and skin and hair had gone. We scooped up what was clinging around the bath and continued cutting up the deer, putting the sections into clear thick bags and then into black bin liner bags so we could take them down in the lift to the van. We carried two bags each and as we looked back, Frankie's mum's bathroom looked like someone had just butchered a six-foot-tall stag deer in it. As we were going back for another two bags, we heard sirens outside and I followed Frankie to his big window. As we looked out, we saw two police cars at the bottom and a fire engine was belting around the corner heading straight for them. We looked at each other and Frankie said, 'We better hurry, there must be a fire in the block.'

We put our T-shirts on and took four black bags each and went down the lift. When the door opened, there were two policemen standing there talking to each other and Frankie thought it was a good idea to talk to them, saying, 'Evening officers, has there been a fire?' The young, serious-looking policeman said, 'We can't say too much, but we have reason to believe that someone has been murdered in the building and we are investigating. Do you live here?' True to form, Frankie puffed out his chest proudly, saying, 'Yes officer, I've lived in this multi all my life. I hope you catch the murderer.'

As we walked out with the prohibited goods hanging off our arms, I said sarcastically, 'Hope you catch the murderer! The murderer is you, you fucking prick! You'll get us the jail yet. Let's get to the van and fucking shut up.' Frankie shrugged his shoulders as if he didn't have a care in the world, and all I could do was shake my head and hope no-one stopped us.

Just as we placed the bags into the back of the van, an ambulance pulled in behind us and we closed the doors and walked back to the lift. There were four firemen standing, looking confused, and Frankie said to them, 'Well lads, what's all the commotion for?'

The fireman said, 'They think someone has been murdered in the bath and the neighbours reported to us that there was a lot of blood running through their plumbing. It's pretty bad. The police said it could be that serial killer that's been going about, and that's all we know at this stage.'

We looked at them and then each other and we put our heads down and walked straight past the police and into the lift. We packed the rest of 'Bambi', and we cleaned the bathroom and stuffed the plastic and shite into the bin shaft. We walked down the emergency stairs, out the side of the multi's concrete columns and away into the darkness. As we walked, I expected a tap on the shoulder that never came.

It was a Saturday afternoon, Mum was working in the pub and I had to go into town to buy a new shirt but my plans changed and I came home early. When I turned the key in the front door and opened it, I heard Mum's songs playing and I wondered why she was home so early.

I threw my bag on the bed at the window and as I walked

to the living room, I could hear laughing and a man's voice saying, 'C'mon Annie, let yourself go.' I immediately went into a state of panic that a man was in our living room. As I walked in, Mum was dancing and she had her head back and was singing along to the song on the cassette player. The man was dancing with his eyes closed and he was stooped forward and snapping his fingers to the rhythm of the beat. I stood there and watched the man for a few seconds and panic turned to confusion and worry at the thought that this man was going to hurt my mum, and I said, 'Mum, what's he doing here?'

Mum was startled as she opened her eyes and said, 'Gary! I thought you were out with your pals. This is Jim.'

'I don't give a fuck who he is,' and I turned to Jim and said, 'Listen pal, you have to go now and don't bother looking at my mum, because if you don't go now, I will knock the fuck out of you.'

Mum told me to leave, and I said, 'I'm not leaving, he is. If he's not gone in two minutes, I'll batter him all the way to the lift,' and I left the room and sat on the edge of my bed until I heard the front door open and close.

I saw my mum pass my bedroom through the frosted glass door, and I heard the sound of the kettle boiling. As it boiled, I calmed down. My mum never said a word to me about what I did, and the flat was silent. She didn't talk to me for two weeks and when she did finally talk to me, she told me how wrong I was and she was right.

It had been years since my dad was gone and the thought of us going through it again sent me into some kind of a psychological state of fear and I immediately went to the worst place possible. What I did was wrong, and I was sorry.

The wind was blowing hard as I turned the corner of the old derelict warehouses that had once been bustling with men and women but now were filled with dust and broken glass and ghosts of something gone. As I made my way to the big steel gates of the meat market, I saw my two pals Bobby and Jock standing just inside the amenities block. As I got closer, they waved me to come over to them, and Bobby said, 'Alright Gary. We were wondering if you were interested in making a few bob with us.'

I was all ears, and said, 'Okay, what are we doing?'

'It's a job for tonight and we need you, so are you in?'

'What's the job?'

Bobby and Jock turned around and nodded towards the busy road where a huge refrigerated articulated lorry was parked, and Bobby said, 'That's the job. Look at the wheels, that truck is packed with boxes of vacuum-packed fillet steaks and tonight we will make a fortune, so we need to know if you're in.'

'Why do you need me?'

Jock said, 'We heard you telling Kevin about the prostitutes in the pub where your mum works and we need you to introduce the truck driver to one of the ladies who will keep him occupied.'

'Okay, I'm in.'

'Right, we'll meet next door in Hungry Mary's later on and we'll need to get the driver in there when he wakes up, so keep an eye when he moves, as there's not too many places he can go and I'm guessing he will want a few pints,' Jock said.

We walked away from each other in different directions and went to work.

That afternoon, Jock was right, and through a casual meeting, as the truck driver arose from the slumber of the front cab of his truck, Jock spoke with him and said he could use our shower in the amenities building and he recommended the shepherd's pie and chips from the pub next door. Jock told him he would see him in there for a pint.

Next up was Bobby. He was to walk into the pub no later than six thirty and he had to do something that was out of character for him and buy somebody a drink, then he was to sit down and talk shite to the driver and Jock until I arrived at seven fifteen. From there, I was to buy a round and talk about anything and everything and then casually throw into the conversation that there were some nice women waiting for a middle-aged, balding, fat truck driver, just ten minutes away.

Jock's plan went to a T and as I was looking over the bar at the Tennent's Lager clock above the spirit optics, it was seven fifty-eight, and this was my cue. The half-sloshed driver didn't need much persuasion, and ten minutes later we left and walked past the old docks and onto the cobbled stones of Exchange Street and into the dingy old bar the women frequented. I stayed for one drink and that was enough and when I left, Dave the truck driver had two women hanging on his every word. I ran up the road and slowed down when I saw Bobby standing there. He may as well have been standing with his two thumbs out and doing a jig next to the truck he was that noticeable. I walked closer and said, 'Could you have not waited across the road in the pub's car park? You looked like you were waiting to rob a truck.'

'Funny cunt. C'mon, Jock will be here in a minute so let's get the seal broke so we're ready.'

Just as we broke the tin serial numbered tag on the back of the wagon, Jock came around the corner and we both stopped and looked in disbelief and Jock flicked the indicator and drove in behind the massive truck. He jumped out of the car and I said, 'Are you taking the piss? I'm new to this but when you see this on the telly, there's always a van and normally it's a big van not a fucking Lada. My mum has a suitcase that's bigger than that boot,' and Jock replied, 'Hurry up, we have a lot to do you cheeky fucker.' As we laughed I said, 'If we don't get the jail this time, next time make sure the Mini is available!'

Bobby lifted the two levers off their cradles and pushed

them up then he pulled open the heavy steel door and it was packed with not premium fillet steaks as we had hoped, but pallets with hundreds of boxes of fish fingers, fish cakes, and crispy pancakes and we looked inside the truck and there was ice-cold steam raging out the door and we all made a face and shrugged our shoulders as we started unloading the goodies from the deep.

We lost count of how many loads we did into the boot and back seat of Jock's car, and we sold crispy pancakes and fish fingers to nearly every pub in Dundee that night. We had made a small fortune and when we got back to the truck, we knew time was wearing on and I said, 'We've made a bit of money so do you fancy getting a few loads for the old age pensioners in the multis?'

Bobby said, 'Yeah right, who do you think we are, Robin fucking Hood. How do you know where the old people live anyway?' and I said, 'Every door in the multis that has the letter A on it, is a pensioner's flat. C'mon, I can't do it without you and it will be good to give back.'

Bobby shook his head and Jock said, 'I'm in, c'mon Bobby, Gary is right, it's a good thing to do.'

'Yeah, c'mon you, you fat fucker, who knows, you might even go to heaven.' And that's what we did.

We delivered boxes of fish to every pensioner's door that had the letter A on it and in the end, as we left the last boxes at the door of 1A Prestwick Court and walked down the emergency stairs, we did feel like Robin Hood and that night changed my way of thinking about Jock's Lada forever.

I walked Bobby and Jock back to the car and said, 'Thanks and I'll see you tomorrow,' and Bobby said, 'It is tomorrow you prick.'

I didn't get much sleep and as I was getting ready for work, I heard my mum talking with our neighbour. 'Morning Mrs Doull how are you, you keeping well?' and the old lady replied, 'Annie, we're fine. Did you get a delivery of fish fingers and those crispy pancakes to your door? There were fish cakes and boxes piled up when I took the rubbish to the bin chute this morning.' I heard Mum saying, 'No, we never got anything, maybe somebody made a mistake. Don't worry about it, I'm sure Jim will eat them. See you later and let me know if you need anything.'

I smiled to myself and got dressed, and then Mum tapped on the glass of my bedroom door and said, 'Gary, are you up? Did you get in late last night? What time's your bus? Do you want a sausage on a roll before you go?'

'Yes I'm up Mum, a sausage roll will be great, thanks.'

'Okay. Mrs Doull was saying that she got a load of fish fingers and crispy pancakes delivered to her door this morning or last night ... bit strange that.'

'I'll be through in a minute Mum. Maybe they made a mistake and got the wrong address.' I could see Mum walking away from the door.

I walked into the kitchen and Mum had the lid of the

chest freezer open and there were boxes of fish bursting out the top. She closed the lid and said, 'Did you not get much sleep last night? You look tired. Have you got the flu coming on?'

'I'm okay, but I'm a bit chesty. I'm looking forward to that roll in sausage.'

Walking to the bus, I hoped we would have a short day as I was thinking about my bed. The bus rounded the corner and I ran across the road and jumped on. I went upstairs as usual and sat in the seat that was close to the stairs. I sniffed and looked out the window as the lights in the tenements started to come to life and I dozed off.

The bus jolted and I woke up and as I looked around, every seat was taken. I coughed unexpectedly and tried to lift my hand up to cover it, but wasn't quick enough and a blob of green, sticky phlegm shot out my mouth, hit the man in front of me and stuck to the bottom of his cap, hanging like an apple on a tree. I looked at the round knob of bacteria and it started to move and form into a teardrop shape as it clung to the man's hat. When the bus moved around the bend, the green blob moved in a synchronised motion. I turned my eyes to the woman sitting next to me and she was busy looking into a tiny round mirror, making sure her eyes were looking tip top.

The bus was packed and beads of condensation were running down the inside of the windows while rain was bucketing down outside. I decided I would try to ignore my phlegm, and I followed a trail of squashed chewing gum remnants on the walls and the roof from years gone by. In the end I had no choice but to stare at the back of the man's head and hope that no-one noticed it and that the man would get up and walk down the stairs, but he didn't, and I was never so relieved to get off a bus in my life.

It was Saturday night and I had been out since five. I had been to a disco in town and had a skin full of lager in me. As I walked up the road, I knew that I would be walking most of the way home as it was either a bag of crispy chips from the Chinese takeaway place, affectionately known as 'The Chinky', or getting a taxi, and I opted to eat and walk. I was in the queue, and I noticed there was a big girl in line, and she was waiting as she propped up the wall. She waved across at me, and I recognised her from school or somewhere. I didn't really know her, but I waved back to be polite.

The girl picked her order off the chest-high counter, and I thought she must have had a few pals outside waiting for her as she had two bags of aluminium containers with white lids, and they were packed with steaming hot Chinese food. As I waited, she left, and after a while, I got my bag of extra crispy chips and I prepared myself for the thought of walking up the road eating cold crispy chips. I walked outside and I saw the girl standing there with her two bags and she was on her own, waiting in a line for a taxi. When she saw me, she shouted over, 'Gary, do you want to share a taxi with me?' and I walked over and said yes. We chatted about where she had been and then the taxi came and when we got in the back seat, she cuddled into me and said, 'This is cosy, eh,' and I smiled. The smell of the Chinese food was making my mouth water and I was starving. As the cab moved the girl started rubbing my leg as she put her considerable head on my shoulder. The smell of fried rice was getting the better of me, so I went along with it. I said, 'Sorry, what's your name?' and she said, 'It's Beverly, like the hills, but call me Bev.'

I nodded, and she took her other hand and brushed across my crotch saying, 'Do you want to come back to my place and we could share some Chinese and whatever else?' I looked at the plastic bag straining to hold all that food in, and I looked at Beverly's dress and it was straining to hold her in, and I said, 'Okay Bev.'

The taxi driver looked in the mirror at me and I shrugged my shoulders and made a face of apologetic defence. The driver shook his head as he pulled into the girl's street.

I jumped out first and she handed me the bag of food and for a second, I thought about running away, but I couldn't as she stuck her hand out of the car and I had to extract her from the taxi's seat. Once Bev recovered from the stress of getting out of the taxi, she took the bags of food then she whispered and said, 'Be quiet as I don't want my mum and dad to know you're here. I've got my key so no talking until we get in the living room,' and I nodded again nervously.

We got through the door and the kitchen was huge and it joined on to an even bigger living room. They had a big TV and two fancy settees and there was a big furry rug along the carpet by the three-bar fire, which was on full blast.

Bev took the food into the kitchen and she came walking towards me and all I could think of was what was in the bag. Her voice changed as she tried to be sexy like the girls in the James Bond films, saying, 'I'll be back in a minute as I'm going to change into something more comfortable,' and I wondered what she was going to wear to make her that comfortable. I couldn't go through with it and I went over to the back door and it was locked so I checked the window in the corner and opened it and I could see the moon had lit up a section of their 'backies'. Any minute now, Bev would be coming down the stairs, more comfortable than when she left, and she would be hungry for more than just fried rice, so I grabbed the bag of food and jumped out the window, and followed the moonlight back through the 'backies' and down to the multis.

I stood in the lift and as usual for a Saturday night, there was shite and piss in the corner, but I was happy to be home. I shared fried rice, sweet and sour chicken and chicken Maryland with my mum, and wondered where I had seen Beverly's face before.

A few months later, fate would bring us back together

again. I was going out with a girl, and we had known each other off and on for a few years. She was a great girl and I really liked her as she was funny and kind hearted.

We were invited to her cousin's engagement party and when we arrived, it was packed with people I didn't know. As we were seated, I looked over in disbelief at the bar and there was a girl that I thought looked like Bev. It was hard to see as there were a lot of people standing around and then the girl at the bar looked over and stared daggers at me and I knew I was in trouble, and I thought to myself oh fuck.

I tried to think but I couldn't as there were no words to explain what I had done. I looked away, and she was looking angrier, and just as I was about to say something to try and get out of this tight spot, Bev headed straight for me and her nose was red and screwed up like a wild animal, and I knew there was nowhere to run.

As she got to the table, she spread her arms out and put her meaty fists down and the table strained and wobbled and she said, 'What did you do with my chicken Maryland?' The girl sitting next to me gave me a puzzled look, and I made a pathetic nervous face and said, 'I ate it,' and before I could offer any more words, she said, 'I'll let you explain to my cousin what a prick you are,' and all I could do was nod and agree. I stood up and couldn't say anything but sorry, and as I walked up the road, I realised I had a lot to learn about right and wrong.

Weeks and months rolled on and the winter was behind

us. One of my favourite comedians, Tommy Cooper, had died on stage and everyone in the audience and in living rooms all across Britain thought it was part of his act and later, it was announced he was gone.

The miners were involved in a bitter conflict to try and stop Thatcher from closing down the pits and flying pickets and police clashed at the gates. Three men lost their lives in a battle that no-one won, and families were torn apart in the process.

Between the gangs, the skinheads, the unemployment, and the unrest and violence in the streets, our city hadn't seen this much turmoil for hundreds of years and it seemed like there was no end to it – and Frankie was on the *Top of the Pops* charts, telling us to 'Relax'.

It was going to be a busy day and as I stood up on the stair platform, sharpening my favourite butcher's knife, there was a row of one hundred sides of beef to be broken down and hung up on hooks.

The sun was shining over the river Tay and into the loading dock. We all had our jobs to do and one of the boss men was standing on the wet concrete floor looking official with his clipboard and pen. As I stood high above everyone else, I noticed a good-looking junior office girl walking across the yard and up the steps to the loading dock. She was carrying an armful of letters, and she was trying to dodge the sides of beef as she was navigating her way to the offices upstairs.

The boss man shouted across the dock at the young girl, hoping we would all be impressed, 'I wouldn't mind her sitting on the end of my cock, eh lads,' and the young girl's face went a reddish colour and she put her head down and walked up the stairs.

A few of the porters laughed, and Bobby and Jock put their heads down in disgust. I walked down the four steps until I stood facing the boss man and I began sharpening my knife, slicing the steel on both sides, and I said, 'Shut yer puss. Do you think you're impressing us or something? She's just a young girl and you're old enough to be her dad.'

He said, 'What did you say to me?' and I said, 'You fucking heard what I said. You should be ashamed of yourself.'

As he took a couple of steps forward, he said, 'Listen to me you prick, do you like working here? You better mind your business, or you'll be out of here.'

I continued sharpening my knife and said, 'I don't want any trouble from you, but I won't listen to shite from you either you fat fucker. Just let me do my job.'

The loading dock had stopped working and everyone was looking through the rails of beef, wondering what was going on. I turned away and put my foot on the step to go up and he shouted over, 'What's wrong with you? What is it, are you a poof? Any more chat from you and I'll take you outside and I'll fuck you myself,'

I had heard enough, and I spun around and threw my long knife as hard as I could at him and it bounced off the concrete making a spark, as the blade flew upwards, missing his head, and I dropped my steel and ran at him. Bobby, Kevin and Jock tackled me and wrestled me into a small fridge under the steps of the offices so I could cool down and after a few minutes, Jock opened the sealed door and said, 'Ignore this prick when you get out, he's not worth it.'

The boss man was sitting down on a folding chair that was far too small for him. When he saw me, he was surrounded by two of his pals and his brother, and he shouted over at me, saying, 'You're a fucking lunatic. You're out of here today. I was only having a joke with the girl. It was a joke! And she didn't hear anything. Pack yer bag and get out of here before we call the police.'

Bobby said, 'You're the boss and no-one wants any trouble, but you messed with the wrong boy, and the wee girl in the office did hear you and so did we. We all heard you,' and the whole loading dock clapped and cheered.

I was staring across at the boss man and Jock said, 'Are you okay? Don't lose your job over this bastard. Look, we're all behind you, so c'mon, let's get a drink and a pie and you'll feel better,' and we walked away. When we got back, I worked harder than ever, and cut down the hundred sides of beef, and from there on in, there was never any more talk about the girls in the office.

Most of us had found a job and with the summer holidays coming up, we all thought it would be great to get the overnight bus down to the seaside town of Blackpool. We put away a bit every week and the countdown was on. None of us had ever been away so when we boarded the bus on the Friday night, we were filled with not just lager, but excitement and thoughts of what the week ahead would bring.

As we passed by the pier, the sea was wild and hundreds of seagulls were flying around and there were people out everywhere. We booked into our bed and breakfast and the landlady greeted us and said, 'Well boys, you'll get a cooked breakfast every morning and dinner is at five every day. There is a cocktail bar just through there and it has a Space Invaders game, and we have a pool table, but we don't have Tennent's lager, but we do have Tetley's, which is just as good. I know you boys will drink anything anyway.

'We have two rules here. Keep the swearing down, and there is to be absolutely no girls allowed in the rooms,' and we all looked around looking for doors and windows to climb in later.

The lady said, 'I can see you're all looking around thinking of ways to sneak girls in here but just so you know, my husband and I take turns staying up all night so you've no chance so don't bother because we don't want to kick you out, okay my loves.'

We dumped our luggage, and the sun was out so we all

put on our Scotland T-shirts and ventured out into this new land. We walked along the long street and there were shops selling 'Kiss me quick' hats and deck chairs, and cockles and muscles, and we bought all three. We heard 'Hi Ho Silver Lining' blasting out a pub and we piled in, and by the time we came back out, like Jeff Beck's song, we were 'everywhere but nowhere baby'. We took our red and white striped deck chairs, and we crossed the street to get to Blackpool beach.

We were all drunk and we weren't the only ones. As we walked along the shelly beach, we could see men herding in donkeys and tying them up to the timber columns of the wharf. As we got to the man with the donkeys, we decided to go for a ride.

Jimmy was too drunk and couldn't get his leg over, so he sat down, and before we left, he was lying down, sleeping on a small hay bale. He looked so peaceful, so we left him there. It was a slow but bouncy journey as the donkeys carried us in protest, and when we got back to the start, Bobby and I were sick on the sand.

Just as we walked over to pick up Jimmy, a donkey let rip with a massive fart and it peed on him. The animal must have been saving this up for a while as it was never ending. Jimmy was oblivious for a while until the animal peed in his mouth then he jumped up as if he was coming out of a nightmare, and we were falling all over the place laughing, as he ran around buckets and spades until he reached the freezing cold water and jumped in.

We wore our hats, but no-one wanted to kiss us, even if it was quick, and we all walked back to the bed and breakfast, and we got to our rooms and fell asleep. All we did was drink and sing about Scotland and try to sneak a girl into our rooms. We had the times of our lives.

When we boarded the bus home, we were all weary, but some were more weary than others, they just didn't know it yet.

We arrived home and I handed out presents of sticks of rock and I bought two birds made out of blown glass that when you pushed the bird, it ducked for water. The next day I was back unloading trucks of beef from Ireland.

We had arranged that we would meet in the pub the following Saturday and when I walked in, Charlie and Bobby were sitting at a low set table with a velvet settee wrapped around it and they were both smiling. As I sat down, Archie and Jimmy were walking out of the men's toilets, scratching themselves, and they both looked very agitated. Jimmy said, 'I'm as itchy as fuck down there and it's driving me mental,' and Archie said, 'Same here. Maybe we're allergic to something,' and I said, 'You've caught something on holiday, and you've brought it back with you.'

They both looked at each other, confused, and Jimmy said, 'How do you mean?' and I told them, saying, 'I have seen this before. The long-distance lorry drivers that deliver beef all over Britain pick up what they call "dirty women" on their travels and I can remember one of the drivers pulling his undies down and showing the boys in the loading dock his 'tadger' and it was crawling with wee beasties called crabs and there was stuff oozing from the end of his nob. It was bad and it scared the shite out of me. From what I can see, you're fucked.'

Bobby said, 'Could you two fuck off and sit over there, you might be contagious,' and Jimmy and Archie looked terrified.

Archie said, 'Fuck me, that's not good,' and Jimmy said, 'Can we die?' and I tried my best to keep a straight face and I said, 'No, you won't die, but your tadger falls off and you can't use it anymore.'

'I'm too young to lose my tadger. I had a good few years of shagging ahead,' said Archie. And I said, 'Not now, you don't, you need to get to a doctor,' and Jimmy went and sat down away from us, and said, 'Fuck me, it's all over.'

I could see another lad walking out of the toilet and he walked towards our table and said, 'What about that fucking Blackpool eh? Hey boys, look at this,' and we all looked at him unzipping his jeans and he pulled out his well-endowed tadger. He was smiling, and he seemed happy with himself, and said, 'Look at this … I've got this green stuff coming out the end of my nob and my mum will see it when she does the washing. I'm fucked,' and he laughed, and we all curled up on the settee in disgust and in unison we said, 'Get to fuck away from us.'

It was a dull Monday morning and Archie and Jimmy sat

at the back of the bus. They smelt of baby powder and as I watched them from afar, they reminded me of the dirty old men with the raincoats in the 'blue movies', as they were scratching like mad under their coats. I went along for some moral support as there was no way I was missing this.

We got off the bus and walked up the road beside the park and as we walked into the sterile white room, the smell of disinfectant was overpowering, and it was making me feel sick.

Archie walked over to the window and said, 'We have an appointment to see a doctor, as we have the flu and we're here to get some medicine.' The woman sitting behind the glass sliding window, said, 'See her over there, she will sort you out,' and we all walked over to this stone-faced nurse who was standing with a clipboard. It was Jimmy's turn to say something. 'Hello there Miss, we were wondering if you could help us, we were on holiday and we caught the flu and we need to see a doctor.' I chipped in and said, 'I don't have the flu, I'm good,' and the nurse smiled a false smile and said, 'You don't have the flu, you have the pox, or the VD, or you've got crabs, so sit over there and fill in the form and wait for your name to be called.'

We walked away, and Jimmy said, 'Hey nurse, there's no need to give us the bad attitude. What about Florence fucking Nightingale and all that. We are the victims here,' and the nurse smiled and shook her head. We took our seats and I looked around the waiting room at a room full of faces that were feeling sorry for themselves.

The following year, we wanted to see a bit of the world, so we went to Spain, which was Blackpool with a tan.

Things were getting crazy at work. People were getting greedy and, other than the scams that had been going on for over thirty years, there were lads coming in the middle of the night with balaclavas on and they had their own sets of keys made. It was so rife and widespread that they were bumping into each other in the dark, as they were emptying the big freezers.

There were lads wearing fishing waders and they would go into the fridges and stuff whole fillet steaks down their leggings. As I stood up on my step platform, I would watch them coming out of the fridge, walking like they had something stuck up their arse. As time passed, the more it got out of hand.

The boss man never talked to me after that day and he had employed a family friend that worked in our crew and he had no idea about the job, as he was brought in to look after the fridges and do the stocktaking. He was a horrible wee bastard who tried too hard to be people's best friends, when it was clear he wasn't.

He marched about with his clipboard, and he would tell everyone, every day, that he was ex-army. No-one cared and we all reminded him that he wasn't in the army now, and that he was a pleb like the rest of us, and he hated the fact that he was.

We all went for a pint after work one Friday, and he was with us. After a few drinks, he started talking about how tough he was and what crazy things he had done. We were sick of listening to him and Frankie winked over the pool table and said, 'I remember I was out with my pals in Spain and one of them dared me to drink a pint of piss and I did it.' Frankie winked again at us, and all four foot of the store man perked up and he said, 'I could do that,' It was like the Punch and Judy show with, 'Oh no you can't', and Frankie pulled out his tadger and filled an empty pint glass, put it on the green cloth of the pool table, and said, 'C'mon then, see if you can do it.' As he walked over and reached for the warm piss, we looked at each other in disbelief. He raised the pint glass up to his mouth and began to drink it and his big thick neck was guzzling down Frankie's waste. When he finished, he smacked the glass on the table and said, 'Right who's next, and we all told him to fuck off and he wasn't happy. He said he would get us back and he stormed out of the pub.

One day, I was just about to leave for the day, and he appeared and said, 'Gary, we got some sausages sent in today so here's your share. I didn't think anything more about it and as I was walking out the gates, he drove up alongside me in his blue Ford Escort, and he reached over and opened the passenger door and said, 'Jump in, I'm heading into town and I'll give you a lift,' and I thought, why not.

As we drove along the road, he kept looking in his mirror and then he slowed down a bit and then a car came out of nowhere and cut him off.

Two men jumped out dressed in suits and I knew then that something was very wrong. My uncle Joe immediately sprung into my mind, and I heard his voice in my head saying, 'Gary, if you ever get caught doing something you shouldn't be doing, never admit to it,' and I took the small package of sausages out of the inside of my coat and placed them on the floor.

I knew this was a set up and the store man was told to do it by the boss man as retribution.

I sat and waited, and the detective opened the passenger door and asked me to get out of the car. I said, 'What for?'

'I want to search you.'

'What are you looking for?'

'We can do this here or at the station.'

I said, 'I've got nothing on me,' and I got out of the car.

The store man sat there in silence as I was frisked and the detective said, 'What's that?' looking at the white butcher's paper parcel sitting on the carpet of the passenger seat.

'It must be his, as it's his car. It's not mine.'

The detective said, 'You're coming with us,' and they took me to the police station. In my head, Uncle Joe was sitting in that room with me, and I said nothing.

After four hours, they let me go and I told Uncle Joe about what happened, and he made a few calls to people he knew and that was the end of that.

When I thought about it, I was relieved that the boss man was stupid enough to get me with only six pork sausages as it could have been a whole different game of retribution. I was glad I was out, and again, it was another lesson I had to learn.

My mum always said to me, 'Son, don't bring the police to this door as we have had enough of them to last the rest of our lives,' and all things considered, I thought I had done not too bad, and I never did bring the police to my mum's house.

CHRISTMAS IN NOVEMBER

When I finished up in the slaughterhouse, I had money put away and the freezer was packed with meat so Mum and I were okay. I got a job driving a forklift and I worked the afternoon shift. Mum had left the watch factory as her time was up using tweezers to put together little pieces of what made watches tick. She was still working with my auntie, and she was now selling scratch lottery tickets on a commission-based gig. Although she was getting older, my mum loved working with my auntie Cath and they both enjoyed each other's company.

I was still training and doing a lot of running and underwater swimming and me and my running partner 'Macko' ran thousands of miles across Scotland together.

Thatcher had wiped her arse with Arthur Scargill's plans for survival, and the men in the collieries suffered badly.

Barry McGuigan had won the World Featherweight title and as he brought his country together as one, Bob Geldof gave us Live Aid and he brought the whole world together, even if it was for only one day.

Industries were redundant and factories were closing down to make way for Thatcher's privatised nation and there were thousands of yesterday's men walking around the schemes and hanging about the shops every day, and I would hear my mum pray for them every night. It was a terrible time and people were doing anything they could to survive and for some, they would try anything to escape this life for a while.

My pal Eck stopped getting the bus to go training with me and he had started on the Evo-stik. After a while, all he did was run around the streets of St Mary's, shadow boxing in a state of euphoria, and he ran until his brain and the glue forced him to collapse, as his nervous system packed in. Glue sniffing was cheap and nasty, and it affected thousands of families like a plague. I used to sit on the stairs and watch as my two pals would be shivering in the corner. They would pour the tan-coloured glue into a plastic shopping bag and make a chimney at the top and grasp it and cover their acne spotted nose and mouth and inhale the fumes in and blow into the bag until their brains were pickled.

They were either jumping about, spinning out, or they

would sit there, slumped against the wall, and their limp hand would fall, and they would drift off into oblivion. Once it got them, they were gone. There would be grown men and women walking about carrying glue in their plastic bags, walking funny and shouting, as paranoia would kick in, and an epidemic was born. Some moved on to inhaling cans of aerosols as they were easily found, but not as easy as the mushrooms.

I would look out my bedroom window from the fifteenth floor and there would be hundreds of people scattered across the vast playing fields, and they would be on their hands and knees looking down at the grass as if they had all lost their girlfriend's engagement ring.

I used to think to myself, 'What the hell are they doing?' and then I found out the fields were teeming with mushrooms, and they weren't the kind you had with your black pudding and square sausage. No, these little grey mini toadstools were sprinkled with fairy dust and LSD, and it seemed like everyone was going along for a ride.

Mum was going across to Fintry to visit my auntie Elen and I went along with her. When we got there, my cousin Jamie asked me if I wanted to go with him and his pals, and because I had been going there since I was a bairn, I knew them all, so off I went.

Jamie said, 'Do you do the mushies Gary? I told him that I didn't, and he said, 'C'mon, you'll get a laugh. We are going up to Billy's house to watch a porno as his mum is out and won't be back for ages.'

The thought of watching a porno with a room full of boys, off their heads on magic mushrooms, sounded very weird, but it was either that or sit at my auntie's window, listening to my mum talk about old times and drinking tea, so I opted for the room full of boys.

We got to Billy's mum's house, and it was like they were all waiting for Jamie to arrive. When we walked into the living room, I waved and said hello around the room.

Billy said, 'Right lads, hand them over. Let's get the good china out. My mum will be out for a while, so we've got till half past ten,' and I thought, that's a lot of shagging.

The plastic bag was sent around the room and Billy said, 'Would anyone like a nice cup of tea chaps?' and they all laughed. Billy put the kettle on and poked his head around the kitchen door, saying, 'One lump or two boys?' They all rubbed their hands and one of the boys put in the video, and I could see the front cover and it had a woman on it with long blonde hair and there was a donkey standing next to her, and I guessed that the porno wasn't set in Blackpool.

The kettle came to the boil as the donkey was being led from a makeshift stable. Billy brought six mugs through on a tray and put it down on the glass coffee table in the middle of the room. I told Billy, 'No thanks, I was daft enough with beer,' and he said, 'You don't know what you're missing.'

He then left and came back with a fancy teapot, that had hot steam coming out the top.

Billy shouted over to one of the boys, and said, 'Pause that TV, this is a good bit. Right, I put eight sugars in there so it should be good, and there's the milk,' and he poured the magic tea into the mugs and the boys drank the lot.

Billy topped up the pot with the kettle and they drank more, and as they drank, the TV was still on pause, and I was glad.

I sat there drinking a bottle of Lucozade and watched and waited. Just as Billy reached across to top up the mugs, the doorbell rang, and we all looked up. Billy looked puzzled and said, 'I wonder who the fuck that is.' As he walked out of the living room, I could see a few of the boys were starting to act funny.

I heard Billy say, 'Mum, what are you doing home, I thought you were at the bingo,' and Billy's mum said, 'I was meant to be, but it was closed. I wasn't bothered, it's been a long day son.' I could hear their voices coming down the lobby, and I looked over at the paused porno, and it looked like the donkey was being milked.

Jamie and his pals were off their heads and I could hear Billy giggle and then they walked into the living room.

Billy's mum said, 'Oh hi lads, what's that you're watching? Is that *Emmerdale Farm*? 'Oooh Billy, a nice pot of tea,' and she reached over and poured the tea into the empty mug on the table. 'C'mon, squeeze over you lot, so I can enjoy my cup of tea,' and as I looked at his mum, my mind was racing.

Billy then disappeared behind the settee and two boys fell on the carpet. They were crawling around trying to find Billy, and my cousin was sitting staring at the TV with his mouth open, trying to work out what button to press on the remote and I thought, 'No Jamie, please no.'

It didn't take long before Billy's mum started to act funny. She was giggling bashfully and had one finger in her mouth, and her face was creased like the wee girl in *The Exorcist*. Jamie finally worked out the remote and got the film to come back on.

I sat there and watched this unfold and couldn't do a thing but laugh. After the film finished, I got them all to stand up and as I stepped over Billy's mum, she had her legs in the air. We walked out and went down to the chipper, dodging spaceships and pink elephants as we walked.

My mum loved Christmas. All through the years, Mum would do whatever she could to make sure that we had a great Christmas. She would go into debt, paying off five different hampers out of the catalogues, and she would spend half the year trying to pay them off before they battered her with interest. Christmas for us would always start in November. Mum would get the tinsel up around every photo frame in the flat, and along the ceiling and around the two doors of the living room and the kitchen. We had a six-foot-tall white-and-silver tree with a big star on the top that lit up and every branch on that tree had a shining bauble hanging off it. There were plastic nativity scenes along the mantelpiece and every year after Guy Fawkes night, our flat would be transformed into Santa's grotto.

I came home from the factory and Mum was putting up the last bits of tinsel and I said, 'Aah Mum, it looks great. You're getting earlier every year but it's great Mum.'

'It's the best time of the year for us son.'

'It is, but don't be going mental again this year, putting yourself in debt. There's no need and we will still have a great Christmas.'

'It's Christmas, stop being a Scrooge, or that ghost will be coming to see you instead of me. Now c'mon, help me with the tinsel,' and I reached over and cuddled her.

I loved going out on long runs through the schemes and as my feet crunched on the frosty grass, I would look at the tenements twinkling with red and orange and green lights, the gold and silver tinsel lighting up the windows in the buildings making them sparkle, and it was magical.

We would go for a drink in the town and in every pub 'Do They Know It's Christmas?' was on, Shakin' Stevens was saying Merry Christmas to everyone, and there was mistletoe hanging at the entrance of the ladies and gents toilets, so if you were lucky, you would get a kiss every time you had to go. Even the gangs called a truce as they all put their Santa hats on.

I always wanted to climb Ben Nevis as it was the highest mountain in Britain, but I never knew where it was or what was involved. My two pals and I left early on a wet Sunday morning and braved the weather. We drove up the long road and got to the bottom of a mass of blackness that was called 'The Ben'. As we rolled down the windows of the Cortina and stuck our heads out, the mountain was moaning at us.

When we got out of the car, we looked up and it was dark and freezing and the sky was a blanket of fog. We looked at each other and started walking. I was wearing a warm coat, jeans and a pair of Adidas Sambas and I felt vulnerable and underdressed for the climb but the other two weren't much better off than me so we kept going. It was hard going but I expected the climb to be worse than it was, and when we got to the top, we only stayed for five minutes as we couldn't see anything in front of us but the snow at our feet. We skidded and fell and slid down the famous mountain track until we got back to the bottom. We agreed to come back and do it again and as we drove down the road from Fort William, we looked out the window at the Scotland we had never seen.

That night, there was a Christmas half-price-cider night on at our local disco and we all walked up the road early so we could get a table near the bar. Two of my pals had taken thirty magic mushrooms each and they ate them like sweeties while we walked. When we reached the front door, the bouncers gave us the once over and said 'in you go' and we were the first ones there. We found a great table near the bar, the toilets and the dance floor, and we got our pints of cider and watched for thirsty-looking girls to walk through the doors.

It wasn't long before the place was busy, and I noticed there were a lot of people acting the same as my two pals sitting next to me. It seemed as if the whole place had been on their hands and knees that day. 'I Wish It Could Be Christmas Every Day' was blasting out the speakers and there were a lot of people getting ready to blast off into space.

I had a few ciders and had to go to the toilet. Huey Lewis was singing about the power of love, and there were two lads smiling at each other, thinking they were Marty McFly hovering into the future, which was a curious thing to see.

I reached the urinal and while I was washing my hands, there was a lad grasping onto his tadger and squeezing the life out of it. He thought it was a hose and he was washing the walls with it. Then suddenly, a voice shouted 'Fire! Fire! There's a fire!' and the spaced-out firefighter went to the rescue with his hose. He ran out of the toilet shouting 'Fire! Fire!' and the whole place went into a mass panic of drug-induced chaos.

My two pals followed the rest of the crowd and ran

outside, and I sat at the table drinking my half-price pint until the real fire brigade showed up and we all went home.

Christmas Eve was a great time for our family. I had two nephews and a niece and I loved seeing their faces light up with excitement as they looked at the bottom of the tree.

My mum 'made' our Christmas with her enthusiasm. She would prepare all the food the night before and we would have a few drinks and stay up until midnight and open one present each while the children were in their beds. We would go to bed around half past one in the morning and be up again as soon as we heard the rustling of the bed sheets, which was always around seven o clock. The presents would be opened with much excitement, and we would tuck into the chocolate selection boxes while breakfast was being cooked. It was magic.

I would always look out the window to see if it had snowed but most of the time, the streets were wet with slush and the cars were glistening with frost. I could hear children's voices saying, 'Thank you Santa' and it was definitely a time of peace and harmony in Dundee, even though it only lasted a few days.

There was prawn cocktail, turkey with all the trimmings, and chipolata sausages, then trifle and blackforest gateau and ice cream and chocolate. It was a day of eating, and we ate so much that by the end of the Queen's speech, none of us could pull a cracker.

New year came and went, and I was glad when it did.

There would be parties, and 'first footing' and people carrying about lumps of coal and boxes of shortie, and calendars, and everyone's auntie's and uncles were singing about bonnie wee lassies. The pubs were all open and everybody was drunk, even before they got to the party, and they would piss in the lift and vomit in your toilet and fall asleep while sitting up straight. There would be people losing their coats on the bed and, for me, the magic that used to be new year was gone. As soon as the clock struck midnight, I looked forward to the year ahead and I hoped it would be better than the last.

THE PHONE CALL
AND THE KNIFE

The new year was over and people's hangovers were in the past. It was back to work for some and back to doing nothing for others. Sam Cooke was in the charts again, telling everyone he didn't know much about anything, and the *Challenger* space shuttle exploded seventy-three seconds after taking off. I stood waiting on the bus and watched through the window of a pub in horror as it burst into flames.

We would all go out on a Saturday night and by now the gangs and the skinheads had all but gone, leaving only a few dozen diehards. Every now and then you would see some of the older but not wiser ones rip into each other for old time's sake. For some, they had nothing else and they just couldn't let it go.

Other than the usual loonies going around, there were the so-called 'standover' men controlling the schemes, who would use fear and intimidation to pick their mark and extort whatever they could from the weak so they could benefit and make a few shillings for themselves. They used young kids as pawns in their game and promised them an easy way out as long as they did what they were told without question. Once they were groomed, they never had a chance, nor were they given one. As they had dived into this life of two bob petty crime, they would be looking over their shoulder every minute of the day, until they got sent away for a spell. When they got out, they became almost legendary in the schemes for being hard men when they were just scared wee boys. Dreams of fast cars and flash women would eventually go, and they would have to settle on three squares a day and their sad reputation, and for them, it was all they had.

I had met a girl and she was like an angel. She worked in the bank, and she was quiet and caring, and although I knew I was punching well above my weight, I really liked her. I asked her if she wanted to go for a drink in the town and when I met her at the bus stop, my heart was excited with butterflies.

We went to a pub that was a renovated church and it had massive high ceilings and all the original beams and architecture were covered in black paint. When we got to the arched door of the church, the bouncers were all standing outside, and I clocked them, ushered the girl through, and we headed straight for the bar. The music was great and just as 'I Died in Your Arms tonight' was playing, all hell broke out. I could see the bouncers laughing and they were throwing chairs and glasses into the crowd, using innocent people as sport, and they were getting badly injured as the wood and glass smashed into their faces.

I grabbed the girl and told her to get down and I wrapped my arms and shoulders around her, while trying to figure a way out. The lads in the gangs were scattered across the pub and they thought they would join in. Before long, there was a flock of pint glasses flying across the room and they all found a target.

I picked the girl up off the floor and put my coat over her head and held her until I got to the emergency exit sign. Just as I kicked the bar on the door, one of the bouncers came running over and I jumped to the side and hit him with a punch that spun him around on his feet.

The girl was screaming and crying as we left, and we walked up the dark lane until we reached the main road. I asked her if she was okay, and she told me she wasn't and she wanted to go home. She was shaking and I held her tight as we walked to the taxi rank. There wasn't anyone waiting and there was one taxi sitting with his light on. When I opened the door, the girl jumped in and said, 'Gary,

I like you, but I don't want to see you anymore,' and she pulled the door shut and the cab moved away, and I never saw her again.

For extra money, I got a job working in a deer factory and the money was good and the boss needed people who could work long hours. It was a twenty-five minute walk and fifteen minutes when I ran from door to door, and I could still get the Saturday off. The worst thing about walking to work on certain days was the smell of burning flesh from the crematorium. I would take a deep breath and run past the chimneys, bellowing with smoke and ash, until I had to breathe again.

Auntie Cath had been asked to manage another pub as The Scouringburn had closed down along with the jute mills. She asked my mum if she wanted to go with her. It was over on the other side of town, and it had a bad name for being rough, but Mum accepted and she told me that if there was anything wrong when she was working there, then she would leave. I was worried as Mum was getting older and had mellowed a lot and she was well past throwing men out the doors of a pub.

I got home from the town and I had bought a new shirt as we were all going out later on that night. Just as I got in the door the phone rang. I thought it would be one of my pals giving me the finer details of the night ahead so I ran to the phone and picked it up.

I said, 'Hello,' and on the other end of the line was a lad I knew from playing in my dad's backies all those years ago, and I had also worked with him a while back. He asked me how I was and what I was up to, and I told him, and he then said, 'Do you fancy getting out of here?' I said, 'What, out of here? Where to?' and he said, 'Australia.'

We spoke for a few minutes and he asked me again, and I said 'Okay, I'm in,' and he said he would be in touch. I put the phone down and Mum said, 'Who was that and what's that you were saying about Australia?'

'That was Steve and he asked me if I wanted to go to Australia with him.'

Mum laughed and said, 'Don't be daft you daft bugger, you're staying here with me. Now c'mon, go and get that nice bit of cod I've made for you.' As I walked into the kitchen I thought about the phone call.

The deer factory could only be described as working in a huge, refrigerated room. It had white walls and big sliding doors that opened out onto even bigger loading docks. Big trucks would bring in hundreds of stag deer and roe deer that had been shot by people who had paid the farmer. They said that they had to be culled as there were too many of them but in reality, these animals were bred for cannon fodder and money.

There were thick plastic benches we all worked from, and there were young girls standing in gum boots and white boilersuits at the tables who would pack the deer into vacuum-packed bags and box them up, and they were sent around the world as venison.

My job was to skin one hundred deer a shift and break them down so the butchers could get them ready to be packed. I would heave and pull and swat away hundreds of maggots as they ate and crawled through the hide, using my elbow and knife to nick the beast until I could find the seam. I would then rip and tear until the deer was bare.

The boss man loved his position, and he would talk down and ridicule the young girls that worked so hard for him. No-one liked him, but he wasn't going anywhere. I bit my tongue every day and I worked harder than everyone else and put away what money I could. Working there was just another means to an end.

It was a long day and night and you had to have a laugh as much as possible. I shouted over to the girls as they packed the deers' tadgers into a bag, saying, 'Well girls, one day somebody might pack the boss man into a bag and send him off to China, as he's the biggest prick in the place,' and we all laughed.

I was watching the TV, and I looked at the kitchen clock and knew Mum was due in any minute from her shift in the pub. I put the kettle on and went to the toilet and brushed my teeth. I could hear keys jingling about as I walked out of the toilet and Mum came through the door. I looked at her and she smiled but it was a smile I knew and had seen before, so I knew something was wrong. 'Hi mum, the kettle's just boiled. Do you want me to make you a cup of tea?'

'I'm fine son, I'm tired and I'm gonna go to bed now.'

As I followed her down the lobby to the living room, she was hunched over and I thought, 'She is getting too old for this.'

'Is everything okay?' I asked. 'Everything okay tonight in that pub? You don't seem yourself.'

She couldn't look at me and she was fiddling about, wiping the top of the clean sink I had washed earlier on. 'What's wrong Mum?'

My heart sank when she said, 'It's okay, and I'm okay, I just want to get a sleep.'

I knew something was very wrong, and I was getting nervous. 'What do you mean, I'm okay, why wouldn't you be okay Mum? So if there's something wrong, you need to tell me,'

'Gary, I'm alright, but there is a man in the pub and he has all these young boys doing things for him and he has young girls sitting on his knee and I think they are on drugs or something. Nothing happened but every time they wanted a drink they whistled on me and at first I ignored them, but the man came over and told me that I worked for him and from now on, I had to serve them free drink every time I was on. I told him I had to run this past Cathy and he said that wasn't a good idea as 'they' wouldn't like that and although he was the boss, he might not be able to control them.

'Tonight, they jumped the bar and took bottles of vodka and whisky, and they took crisps and nuts as they were having a party after closing time. The man said if I said anything, I would be in trouble.'

I looked at my mum and she was getting upset. I held her hand and she was shaking, and I was struggling to control myself.

I said, 'You're not going back there. What's the man's name?'

'Don't you do nothing daft.'

'What's his name?'

'I can't leave Cathy and I need the money. I'll tell Cathy and we will sort it out.'

'Mum, there's no sorting this out. These people are leeches, and they prey on people and suck the life out of them. You can't go back. Did any of them touch you? Tell me the man's name.'

'Gary, he is a hard man, and everyone is scared of him so stay away from him, I'm telling you,' and I told Mum everything would be okay, and I hugged her and thought about what I was going to do.

It was a long night, as I lay there, looking up from my bed out the window at the floodlight at the top of the multi. I knew what I wanted to do, I just needed to think about it. I tossed and turned and dozed off. I had a violent dream, and my dad was there but it was me, and a man was gurgling blood and my dad was on top of him, but it was me that was doing all the damage, and then I woke up and my pillow was soaking, and it was cold and wet.

The next day, I asked my pal to meet me at the bottom of my block. I was in a daze as I was looking at the children playing in the park on the hill and then, as usual, my friend jumped out on me, like a ninja trying to scare me. 'What's up with you, you fucker, you sounded funny on the phone, everything okay?'

I told him what had happened, and he said, 'Let's get a couple of hammers and go down there and we'll see how hard these bastards are. Who is he? Do you know him? What's his name?'

'It doesn't matter what his name is, or who he thinks he is, I don't give a fuck. Nobody is gonna stand over my mum, or bully her. They are a bunch of wannabe gangsters and I need to sort it out. I knew you would want to help but the more I think about it, it's better I do this myself. I'll phone you if I need help,' and he smiled and disappeared through the concrete court and into the woods.

I walked to the lift, and I knew what I had to do. As I lay in my bed that night, I listened to my mum praying for Auntie Cath and I also got a mention. I doubted if anyone would be praying for the standover man in the pub or the young thugs he controlled, and even if there was, he was going to need more than a prayer to save him.

I asked around and went down to the pub where my mum and auntie worked, and as I walked in, he was sitting there on the red settees. It was just as Mum said, he had seven young boys scattered between three tables, looking tough, and there were two skinny young girls with short skirts on hanging off the man with the sheepskin coat and the furry collar. As he rubbed a girl's leg, I knew who he was and what he was. He was an ugly man inside and out and I could see how much he loved his position as the king of this concrete jungle. He sat there encouraging and thriving on fear and violence so he could take the lion's share and leave these toothless cubs to fight over the scraps.

I stood at the end of the bar and drank my pint until I had seen enough and I left.

I went down again for a look around and to familiarise myself with the streets and a place to hide and I knew then, I was ready.

I took my bowie knife from the side of my bed, wrapped it in a dish cloth and put it in a plastic bag then I called a taxi. The taxi flicked his front lights on and I walked to the cab and jumped in and asked the driver how his night was. We talked about the Russians and the Chernobyl nuclear disaster and Peter Gabriel was on the radio. As the song finished, I told the driver to pull over and I paid him and jumped out two streets back from where the pub was.

The streets were dark and there was no-one around. There was an orange ambience from above as I passed each light pole. I stepped into the closie and darkness and my knife were my only friends. I looked out in the dark at every person that went into the pub, and watched them stagger out a few hours later. Time escaped me as I focused on the door of the pub, and I kept saying to myself, no-one will bully my mum again.

The door pulled inwards and there he was. He was on his own and as he walked, he was pulled to the side of the kerb, as the drink and his legs betrayed him. I took my knife out of its sheaf and followed him along the road. As he slowed down, I sped up and grabbed him with every bit of me and pushed him into the black fence. I crushed the soft lapel on his coat and put my bowie knife's razor-sharp blade under his Adam's apple. He froze in fear and he was wide-eyed and confused, and he said, 'What the fuck! You have the wrong man pal!'

As I steadied myself, I said, 'Shut it you. I have the right man. I've been watching you and I know you. You know the two old women that work behind the bar?' and he blinked his eyes and stared at me. I tightened the blade and stared back and said, 'So you do. Well, if I ever hear about them getting any trouble from you or yer pals in that pub again, I will come back to see you and the next time, I will cut your fucking head off, do you understand?'

I tightened my grip on his lapel and pressed the knife on his neck, and he said, 'I understand, don't cut me,' and I looked at him and banged his head on the fence as hard as I could and I stood back a couple of steps and gripped my knife and stared at the 'hard man' as he slumped down the railings of the fence.

I walked away, got to the corner, stepped into the dark closie and into the backies then I jumped the fence and ran over a patch of grass and through a children's play park that led to the main road. I flagged down a taxi and jumped inside and thought about my mum.

When I got home, Mum was still up so I stuck my head around the glass door and said, 'Hi Mum, I thought you would be in bed,' and she said, 'I couldn't sleep, so I'm having a cup of tea. I'll be going in a minute. Where did you go tonight?'

'I was out with Kev.'

'Be careful with him, that boy would fight his own shadow.'

I smiled and said, 'He has a good heart and he is a good pal. I'm going to bed. Everything will be alright. Get a sleep. Goodnight Mum.'

I went to my room and got ready for bed. I thought about the man and wondered if he would tell anyone about what had happened to him, but I already knew the answer. He couldn't, as if he did, his reputation as the 'man' would be diminished, and if word got out, then he would be well and truly finished.

LOVE AND LEAVING

A couple of months had passed since that night and there was no more trouble in the pub but I still asked Mum every night she went to work if everything was alright. I was coming out of my room one Sunday morning and I heard my mum talking to our neighbour and they were talking about me going to Australia. I stood at the corner and listened. 'Annie is Gary still going to Australia? It's just that I've not heard you speaking about it and I've not seen Gary for a while.'

'Fran, he has been working every hour under the sun in that deer factory and that's how you've not seen him. He hasn't mentioned it for a few months so I don't think he is going anymore. He won't leave me.'

As soon as I heard that, my eyes filled and my stomach

was in knots. Fran said, 'I hope he doesn't go Annie, he is a good laddie.'

My mum said, 'He is making a bit of money and he won't leave us,' and then they said cheerio to each other and Mum came inside.

I thought about it all day , pacing my bedroom and trying to think of the words to say to her, but I couldn't, so I left the bedroom and walked into the kitchen where Mum was standing making her homemade soup. I said, 'Mum, I need to speak to you,' and she looked at me with her worried expression I had seen too many times.

'What's wrong son?'

'It's about me leaving and going to Australia.'

She looked at me with a nervous smile and said, 'You're not really going are you?'

'I am Mum. I need to go and give it a try because if I stay here, I'll end up like him.'

'You will never be like him, so if that's the reason you're wanting to leave, then you don't have to.'

I could see she was starting to get upset and I was getting a fizzing feeling in my throat as I said, 'It's not just him, but I know he is in me and I'll get in trouble if I stay here and don't try somewhere else. I want to go and if it doesn't work out, I'll come home.'

Mum's face started to contort and all I could see was a picture of pain, and she put her head down and reached out to me and said, 'I'm going to miss you,' and she cried and I cuddled her tight and listened to her crying into my chest. I couldn't talk as the lump in my throat was too great, and my mum looked up at me, and as she held my face, suddenly I was eight years old again, and she said, 'My boy ,my laddie'.

As the months went by we never talked about me going away and I was glad. The thought of leaving was too hard so we kept going and Mum prepared herself by telling the neighbours and they would remind me every time I saw them at the lift.

Pat the 'rat' had been living across the landing from us for years and on occasions, I would help him up from the corners of the walls at the bottom of the multi, as he used me as a crutch after one of his sessions on the drink. Pat was a 'scaffie', and he had been emptying people's bins all his life. He lived on his own and had a Bill Haley hairstyle and orange-rusty nicotine fingers. There was decades of filth trapped under his big thick nails, and as he smiled, there were always bits of food stuck between his dilapidated teeth. Pat liked my mum, and through the years, he was always sniffing around and Mum used to give him soup, particularly in the cold months of winter. Depending on how drunk he was, Pat sometimes took Mum's kindness as a sign of something else and she would send him on his way.

As soon as he got wind I was leaving, he left a few flowers on the landing doorstep and then he left a box of Black

Magic chocolates. He was a nice enough man but I could never find out why he had that name and there was no way he would be knocking on my mum's door, bothering her with cheap sweeties and daffodils when I was on the other side of the world. The next time I saw him, I had to tell him once and for all that *Love Thy Neighbour* was just a program on the TV.

Christmas was only days away and as I lay in my bed, I thought about a lot of things and, most of all, I thought about my mum. I was leaving her, and I wouldn't be meeting her at the shops to carry the shopping, and I wouldn't be keeping her company in the noisy shared laundry down at the bottom of the lift, or carrying the washing, or listening to her stories from the pub, or listen to her call Thatcher for everything, and I wondered where I was going and what I was going to do when I got there, but most of all, I thought about how much I was going to miss her.

It was Christmas Day and all I could do was stand back and watch in silence at what was going on. I listened to everything as they ran about doing what they always had done and I realised I loved them with all my heart and soul. I never had much but I had them and soon, I would be leaving them. As I looked at them they were happy and noisy. Mum was micromanaging the oven and swigging on her Carlsberg Special, and my brother-in-law, Jake, was tidying up the torn Christmas paper that was abandoned everywhere, and the smell and the atmosphere were too overwhelming. I went to the toilet and sat on the edge of the seat and thought about leaving and I came out and had to be brave again. It was the best and the worst Christmas I ever had.

It was now 1987 and with only a few days to go before I left, we all went out for a drink and there was a comedian on at the local working men's club. As always, comedians were followed around by strippers so we decided to go along for a laugh and a bit of titillation. The place was packed and we managed to get a good table close to the bar and we sat there drinking and talking about old times. The beer was going down better than the comedian's jokes, and every time we went to the bar, we had to go in two' to help get the drinks back without spilling them.

It was my pal's round and I thought I would give him a help. Harry had the voice of an angel but he had such a bad stutter that he couldn't put out a sentence to save himself. I used to tell him he should sing when he spoke and he could be Dundee's first rapper and he said, 'F … F … Fuck off you c … c …' and we would laugh.

We stood at the bar and the moaning puss of a barmaid said, 'What do you want?' and Harry said, as he desperately tried spitting out the words, 'Thhhh-three p-p-pints of l-l-lager and t-t-t-two pints of h-heavy and three p-p-pints of sp-p-p-p … fuck it, m-m … make it six p-p-pints of lager,' and the barmaid repeated the order and we took the two trays back to the table and no-one noticed.

The stripper came on and she made the comedian's jokes the highlight of the night. By the end of the night I can't remember saying goodbye to my pals I had grown up with in the schemes.

The day I was dreading arrived and I packed my bag and it sat in the corner of my bedroom, ready to go. As I looked around at the walls I wasn't sure if I was. My mum booked a taxi and she said, 'Right son, it's time to go.'

I told Mum I had to go to the toilet and for her to go down to the bottom so the taxi wouldn't drive off. Mum left and I didn't go to the toilet. I went into the kitchen, the living room, and the toilet and I stood at my mum's bedroom door and looked in and wondered when I would be back.

I thought about what we had been through together all those years and I picked up my bag and stood at my front door and stared at the letterbox and the chains on the door. I walked out into the landing and the neighbours were waiting at their doors and 'Pat the rat' waved at me and cried as I went into the lift.

I got to the bottom of the multi and there was an icy wind blowing through. Mum was waiting in the cab and as I opened the door she said, 'We thought you fell down the hole,' and I jumped in and the taxi drove off.

The taxi arrived at my sister's house and as we got out, the front door opened and they were all looking at me as I grabbed my bag. We got inside and there was a strange atmosphere in the house and Jake tried his best to keep the mood jovial as he put on some music. The TV was on in the background and the central heating was blasting. We had a few drinks and ordered pizza and we were all saying everything and nothing, as the clock was ticking.

I followed my niece and two nephews up the stairs to their room and I said, 'I wanted to talk to you about me going away. I am going to miss you. Never forget I love you. You know, I'm not going forever and I'll write you postcards. Look after your wee sister. Now c'mon, give yer uncle a cuddle' It was hard to control my emotions.

My mum was unusually quiet and every time I looked at my sister, her glasses steamed up and the tip of her nose went red and she started to cry. There was a weird sensation of dread I had never experienced before as my brother-in-law said, 'Gary, the taxi will be here in five minutes, so we should be moving downstairs.' As we walked, the room closed in and the atmosphere changed and I was hit with the realisation that I was going, and he said, 'Look after yourself over there. We will be okay here. I'll miss you,' and then as we got to the bottom of the stairs, the taxi peeped it's horn.

I opened the door and Jake took my bag, and said to the taxi driver, 'Alright pal, cold tonight. Just give us a minute to say cheerio.'

I looked at my niece and nephews and we had a group cuddle and my sister was crying and I could see my mum in the background waiting. I gave my sister a big cuddle and she couldn't talk. I hugged my brother-in-law then I walked to my mum and she was crying and her face was contorting and I hugged her and I didn't want to let her go.

My heart was breaking, and I couldn't say anything. Mum looked at me as the tears ran down our faces and she whispered in my ear, 'Son, work hard, don't forget about me. Don't come back son, there is nothing here for you. I know that now. I'll pray for you every night.' I looked at her and I couldn't find the words to say goodbye.

I jumped in the back of the taxi and looked out the side window. They were all huddled together and as they waved, the taxi drove off. I looked out the window and I couldn't get rid of the lump in my throat. I saw the driver looking at me in his mirror and there was silence as we drove through the dark empty streets to the train station.

The taxi pulled in and the driver jumped out and went to the back of his car. I wiped my face with the sleeve of my coat and he handed me my black holdall bag and said, 'Where are you off to son?' and I said, 'Thanks, I'm going to Australia,' and he said, 'Australia eh! Watch out for those crocodiles,' and I smiled and put my bag down on the ground.

The taxi drove off and I stood there, looking around. The cobbled stones were all slippy and sparkling with frost, the wind groaned and fog crept through the gaps in the wharfs of the old docks. I turned around and looked at the buildings and the shops of the city I grew up in, and the place was deserted.

Just as I was thinking that there was no time for doubt, I heard a voice shouting through the fog, 'Hurry up, the train's coming Gary,' and I picked up my bag and put it over my shoulder and ran to the railway bridge and down on to the platform. As I stood there, I could see the lights of the train in the distance and I knew I had to keep going and catch the last train to London, and in the morning I would be on my way to Sydney, Australia.

AFTERWORD

My mum will always be in my thoughts. I have a photo of our council flat in the multis where we lived and I feel lucky to have it. It's where we loved and laughed and cried and it's where we struggled and it's where we kept going on with the mindset that things would get better even when they didn't.

Living there gave me the resilience to persevere in life and try to be the best I could be with what I had in me. After all these years, it's still my home. It's the place where I felt I belonged. Even though the multis were turned to dust years ago, the memories still remain.

A lot of years have gone by and there has been a lot of water that has flowed under the bridge, and in life, some of us take the high road and some of us have taken the low road, but no matter what road we take, we should never forget the road we came on.

I will never forget those years in my life, or my mum, and what she endured and what she did every day. Other than a few old photos, that is all I have of her. We were poor and we struggled every day but she never gave up and without me knowing it, she taught me never to give up.

I wrote these words for my family as I wanted them to understand that life can be tough but you just need to keep going. I wrote this book for my mum as she deserves to be remembered.

Someone once said to me referring to my life in Dundee, 'Well it wasn't exactly the Bronx now, was it?' and at the time I thought it wasn't worth answering. As for the person that made the bold statement, I used to wipe his arse as a baby so what the fuck did he know anyway.

Writing about boxing has always been a passion of mine but writing *Annie's Boy* was different on so many levels. This was my life and every word came from my heart and my mind, as I had to go back through every year in my head and relive it all over again. Certain events and the music helped me.

I remembered the smells, the sights and the sounds as if it was yesterday. It was a very emotional journey for me to tell this story but I think it is an important story to tell about living with the mindset that you have to keep going, even when life knocks you down.

Gary Todd lives in Sydney, Australia and he lives happily with his wife, Jenny and they have three children, John, Erin, and Hannah. He is an international best-selling author with his two books, and he is involved in the sport of boxing as a trainer, cut man, and a writer, and he is highly regarded as an expert analyst of the sport around the world. He earns a living as a construction boss.